Contents

Title: The Trillion Dollar Problem
Authors: Clive Hays, Charlene Newton, Neil Hays

Published by:
Clover Framework Ltd
Elgin, Scotland
www.cloverframework.io

First Edition: Marchl 2024

ISBN: 9798320112008

Printed in the United Kingdom

CONTENTS

1. **OUR WHY** (PAGE 7)
   - OUR WHY

2. **HOW TO USE THE WORKBOOK** (PAGE 9)
   - HOW TO USE THE WORKBOOK
   - TIME COMMITMENTS
   - CLOVER DIAGRAM

3. **INTRODUCTION TO CLOVER** (PAGE 15)
   - THE CLOVER FRAMEWORK: YOUR ROADMAP
   - EMPLOYEE ENGAGEMENT AND ITS RELATIONSHIP TO PROFIT
   - WHAT IS EMPLOYEE ENGAGEMENT?
   - THE STATS DON'T LIE
   - NOT JUST FOR HR
   - A JOURNEY NOT A DESTINATION
   - THE 3 LAYERS OF ENGAGEMENT
   - WHY IT MATTERS

4. **COMMUNICATION** (PAGE 25)
   - WHY IS COMMUNICATION CRITICAL?
   - 14 KEY WORKPLACE COMMUNICATION STATISTICS

- How to Model Communication
- How to Coach Communication Practices
- How to Reward Communication
- How to Celebrate Communication
- How to Sustain Communication
- How to Rescue Failing Communication
- Communication Exercises and Worksheets

5. Learning (Page 61)
   - Why Is Learning Critical to Employee Engagement?
   - How to Model Lifelong Learning
   - How to Coach Learning Practices
   - How to Reward Learning
   - How to Celebrate Learning
   - How to Sustain Learning
   - Learning Exercises and Worksheets

6. Opportunity (Page 83)
   - Why is Opportunity Critical to Employee Engagement?
   - How to Model Opportunity Practices
   - How to Coach Opportunity Practices
   - How to Reward Opportunity Gains

- How to celebrate Opportunity gains
- How to sustain opportunity gains
- how to rescue opportunity losses
- The role of Prioritization & Purpose
- Opportunity Exercises and Worksheets

7. **Vulnerability (Page 121)**
    - Why is Vulnerability important to engagement
    - How to Model Vulnerability
    - How to coach vulnerability
    - How to reward vulnerability wins
    - How to celebrate vulnerability
    - How to sustain vulnerability
    - how to rescue failing vulnerability practices
    - Exercises and activities to build trust and openness

8. **Enablement (Page 155)**
    - Why is Enablement critical to engagement
    - How to Model Enablement
    - How to coach enablement
    - How to reward enabled workers
    - How to celebrate enablement gains
    - How to sustain enablement

- How to rescue failing enablement practices
- Exercises and worksheets for enablement

9. Reflection (Page 189)
    - Why is Reflection critical to engagement
    - How to Model reflection
    - How to coach reflection
    - How to reward reflection
    - How to celebrate reflection
    - How to sustain reflection
    - How to rescue Floundering reflection
    - Reflective exercises for individuals and teams

10. Appendix (Page 231)
    - Worksheets, tools, and resources for implementing the CLOVER framework

11. References (Page 243)

12. Index (Page 245)
    - An index of topics covered in the book for quick reference

OUR WHY

Human beings need to stay competitive. Our competitive advantage is our ability to work together. When that works, it is incredible what can be accomplished.

When culture thrives, employees are more engaged, teams are more cohesive, and businesses thrive due to being more resilient.

Engaged employees are more productive, more likely to stay with their employer, and more aligned with the company's goals.

 ## To Use This Workbook

Your Engagement Workbook: Welcome to your Field Guide to a Happier, More Productive Workplace

Okay, so here's the deal: No matter your level in the organization, think of this as your engagement cheat sheet for building an awesome workplace. Senior leaders can apply our engagement practices with their team of managers. These same managers can apply it with their teams. This isn't a textbook, it's your engagement toolkit. To get the most out of it, here's the approach we suggest:

1. **Do Your Homework:** It's tempting to skip to the action, but spend some time getting to know CLOVER. It's your foundation for understanding *why* certain things improve engagement and *how* to practice these things to impact your organization day-to-day.

2. **Follow the Yellow Brick Road:** Okay, the workbook's not *that* magical, but it IS laid out in a specific order. Don't skip around too much, as each part builds on the last

one. Think of it as leveling up – start with "Communication" and work your way to "Reflection."

3. **The Activities Aren't Just Busywork:** Think of our worksheets like a workout for your engagement muscles. Doing them is what takes this from 'cool ideas' to actual results. "Worksheet C1: The Communication Audit" sounds boring, but it's where you figure out how to really improve how your company talks to itself. That stuff MATTERS.

4. Look out for the **Grab Your Compass** and **Hit The Pause Button** Icons at the end of each chapter. They guide you to weekly and monthly plans in the Appendix. We have learned these plans help you practice the skills you've just read about AND they make sure you don't forget something that seems "less important" now but impacts long-term engagement. Use them for ready-made structure, even if you need to adjust them a bit to suit your organization.

You're not gonna nail this on the first try. These practice sections are about taking stock: seeing what works, fixing what doesn't, and giving yourself some credit for what you've accomplished. This is how you get GOOD at engagement, not just okay.

5. **Steal Ideas (the Legal Kind):** Our case studies are there to fuel your brain. How did company X use better communication to reduce turnover? Can you adapt that to YOUR situation? This section is full of cheat codes. Use them!

How To Use This Workbook

6. **Become a Nerd (Optional, But Helpful):** We've tossed in a few Bonus Sections for all you overachievers out there. This stuff isn't *required*, but it's super useful if you're dealing with a tricky problem or just love learning about how great organizations are built.

7. **The 'Never Quit' Mentality:** Engagement isn't a box to check off, it's a way of running your business. You might need to revisit the workbook, adjust, or try again later. It's totally normal! Every time you circle back, you're a bit smarter and a bit more equipped to lead the charge.

Time Commitment Expectations

How Much Time Will It Take?

The estimated total time commitment for this workbook is between 6-8 hours. However, this isn't a race. Quality trumps speed.

Pro-Tip:

Split the 6-8 hours into manageable chunks spread over a week or a month, depending on your pace. This makes the commitment less daunting and the process more enjoyable.

Bottom Line:

Your investment in completing this workbook is also an investment in yourself and your team. Go into it with an open

How To Use This Workbook

mind, stay committed, and don't hesitate to revisit sections as you evolve in your engagement journey. You've got this!

We can show you *how*, but YOU have to DO the work. If you're genuinely focused on creating a place where people want to be, where every contribution feels valued – this workbook is your roadmap. Now, let's roll up our sleeves and get started!

Introduction

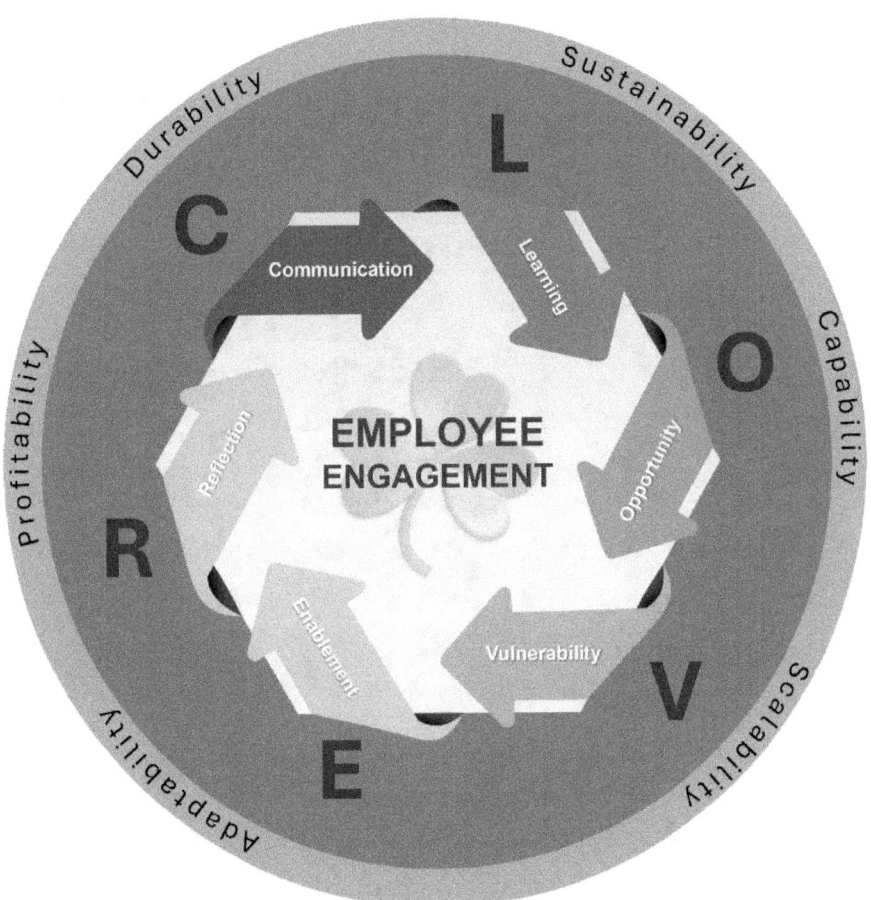

INTRODUCTION

The CLOVER Framework:

Your Roadmap to a Truly Engaged Workplace

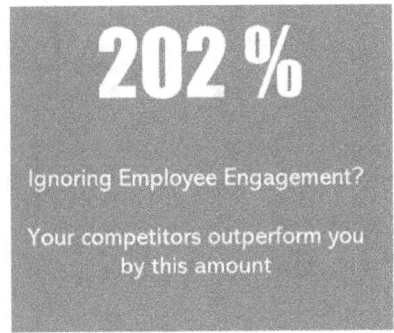

While it's easy to dismiss engagement as a 'soft metric,' its impact on hard business outcomes is undeniable.

Gallup estimates low employee engagement costs the global economy **$7.8 trillion in lost productivity - that's 11% of global GDP.**

Introduction

Employee Engagement and Its Relationship to Profit

59%
Lower Turnover

High levels of engagement can reduce turnover by up to 59%.

17%
More Productive

Engaged employees are 17% more productive than their disengaged counterparts, according to Gallup.

Employee engagement is more than just a buzzword; it's critical to your organization's success.

Engaged employees are more productive, more likely to stay with their employer, and more aligned with the organization's goals. Research consistently shows a direct correlation between higher levels of employee engagement and profitability increases, higher customer satisfaction (including NPS scores), and reduced turnover rates (higher eNPS scores).

Introduction

What Is Employee Engagement?

First things first: Employee Engagement is not synonymous with job satisfaction, nor can it be reduced to employee happiness. It's a multi-dimensional concept that includes emotional and intellectual commitment to an organization. An engaged employee is not just satisfied and happy, but also emotionally invested in the company's mission and vision.

The Stats Don't Lie

For those still skeptical about prioritizing employee engagement, consider this: Organizations with highly engaged teams are 21% more profitable, according to a Gallup study. Think it's an HR issue? Think again. Engagement impacts everything from customer satisfaction to the bottom line, making it a business issue everyone should care about.

Not Just for HR

Despite the statistics and obvious benefits, why do some businesses still consider employee engagement an "HR issue" to be siloed away from the broader objectives of the organization? Perhaps it's a lack of understanding, or perhaps it's the assumption that it requires too much effort for too little immediate return. Both assumptions are incorrect and dangerous for the long-term viability of a business.

A Journey, Not a Destination

Engagement isn't a one-time project; it's an ongoing process of improvement. It's an investment in your employees and by extension, in your company's future. It's about crafting a workplace environment where employees feel heard, valued, and, most importantly, engaged in the work they are doing.

The 3 Layers

Look for signs of engagement at each level:

- **Emotional Engagement:** Your employee's emotional attachment to their job, team, and company drives passion and enthusiasm.
- **Intellectual Engagement:** Your employees are fully absorbed by, and enthusiastic about their work, leading to improvements in the quality of your professional output.
- **Behavioral Engagement:** Employees are behaviorally engaged when they add discretionary efforts to their work, such as taking on additional responsibilities without being asked.

Why It Matters

While it's easy to dismiss engagement as a 'soft metric,' its impact on hard business outcomes is undeniable:

Increased Productivity: According to Gallup, engaged employees are 17% more productive than their disengaged counterparts. This is an exponential number – the cumulative effect of each individual reaching this mark is significantly larger for the whole organization.

Lower Turnover: High levels of engagement can reduce employee turnover by up to 59%.

Higher Customer Satisfaction: Companies with engaged employees outperform their competition by up to 202%, a fact supported by multiple studies.

The Domino Effect An engaged employee affects more than just their own performance. Their enthusiasm and commitment to quality at work can serve as a morale booster and model for the team. They are more likely to collaborate with other team workers and if they have a best friend at work, they are 2x as likely to highly recommend their company to friends and less likely to leave. On the flip side, a disengaged employee can sour the collective spirit and productivity of a team. The domino effect of engagement or disengagement can either propel a business forward or hold it back significantly.

Introduction

A Business Imperative

Given the far-reaching impact of employee engagement on productivity, customer satisfaction, and overall business success, paying attention to it is a business imperative.

> Ignoring employee engagement is like leaving $$$ on the table, or worse, leading your organization to failure.

Our Solution: The CLOVER Framework

Think of the **CLOVER** Framework as your GPS for creating a work environment where people aren't just there for a pay check; they're excited to be part of something bigger. **CLOVER** is not about isolated change initiatives – it is all about the interconnected practices that make people feel valued, motivated, and genuinely eager to contribute. Let's break it down letter by letter:

- **Communication:** We all know talking is important, but workplaces need more than chatter. CLOVER-style communication is about connecting with purpose and building real understanding, where trust is high enough that every voice in the organization knows it'll be heard, even when opinions differ.
- **Learning:** In a world that changes fast, learning keeps your team adaptable. It's not just about fancy training programs – it's a mindset that says professional development is vital and mistakes are a chance to grow.

If your organization isn't focused on learning, its future is uncertain.

- **Opportunities:** Humans are not meant to fit a static job description. Humans thrive when they have opportunities to grow and contribute beyond the organization's initial job description. Give people room to test out ideas, step up into leadership, and be a part of building the organization's future. When you don't offer opportunities, top performers walk out the door.

- **Vulnerability:** Think of Vulnerability as creating a culture where saying "I don't know" or "I need help" isn't seen as weakness. Vulnerability fuels trust. It breaks down barriers, strengthens teams, and let's be honest, sometimes it's how the most innovative solutions are found.

- **Enablement:** It's frustrating when you're expected to do great work but don't have the right tools, training, or support, and even more frustrating when organizational processes get in the way of getting stuff done. Enablement goes beyond the basics – it empowers people to make the right decisions, be accountable for team and organizational goals, and make a measurable difference in meeting them.

- **Reflection:** Hitting the pause button might seem old-fashioned, but it's essential. Whether it's individuals taking a personal "lessons learned" moment or organization-wide reviews, reflection is what helps you course-correct and continuously improve. Otherwise, you're going in circles, duplicating mistakes, and not making real progress.

Some high-level questions for your reflection:

1. Communication: How well does your organization communicate at various levels?
2. Learning: What are your current learning and development programs?
3. Opportunity: Are there avenues for growth and advancement within the organization?
4. Vulnerability: How safe do employees feel in showing their authentic selves?
5. Enablement: Are your team members empowered to make decisions?
6. Reflection: How often does the organization take time to reflect on its practices?

So, Why Invest in the CLOVER Framework?

It's not a warm-fuzzy exercise in niceties; this is about building a stronger, smarter organization. Each part of CLOVER is a vital piece of the employee engagement puzzle from communicating the WINs of an engaged team to reflecting on how we can do it better tomorrow. The results are measurable: boosted productivity, loyal employees, happier customers. . . you get the picture. CLOVER makes your life as a leader (and employee!) much easier and a lot more fun!

Wait, Before You Dismiss "Employee Engagement" as a Buzzword...

Introduction

...let's talk numbers. Because here's the thing: this isn't some vague "HR issue." There's solid data linking good engagement to higher profits, low employee turnover, and even rockstar-level customer service. The best companies know their people are their #1 asset and invest accordingly.

The Thing to Remember

Engagement isn't some grand project – it's a mindset shift. It's how you run your day-to-day, communicate with your team, and design and grow your company culture. The CLOVER Framework is your guide to laying the foundation for a workplace people genuinely want to be a part of, which pays off big time for everyone involved.

Fun sidenotes on the CLOVER acronym:

Why isn't our framework called VELCRO? We had decided on the important practices for our engagement framework and knew the starting letters of each practice. We didn't stick (pun intended) to Velcro, our first idea, and chose CLOVER because of its happy, refreshing image and desirable traits. Clover rejuvenates soil as a nitrogen-fixer. We want to rejuvenate organizations as an engagement-fixer! And just as Clover grows like a weed, employee engagement spreads fast once it is planted!

Let's plant some CLOVER in your organization! Are you ready to fix engagement in your workplace?

Let's start with the C for Communication!

Communication

Why Is Communication Critical to Employee Engagement?

Would it surprise you to hear the single most important habit a manager can practice is to engage their employees in at least one meaningful conversation each week?

Meaningful communication builds relationships among leaders, managers and colleagues at work and is a high predictor of productivity, performance, and happiness on the job. Let's get on with it!

By some counts, leaders can have as many as 400 touchpoints with fellow employees every day! How can we make sure these touchpoints make workers feel they belong? How can we add purpose to their workday by connecting their personal work to the higher purpose of your organization?

For starters, try this simple checklist to make your next weekly 15-30 minute touchpoint with an employee meaty, connected to purpose, and actionable:

- ☐ Provide a quick timely update(s)
- ☐ Share why weekly check-ins are important to you
- ☐ Connect their work to the purpose of the organization
- ☐ Take time to build the relationship
    - o Ask about the family: celebrations, health, etc.
    - o Check-in on Work/Life Balance
    - o Check-in on stress level and stress management
    - o Check-in on impacts of recent changes
- ☐ Recognize a strength
- ☐ Ask about a current challenge
- ☐ Ask how you can support them
- ☐ Focus on their individual interests and growth goals
- ☐ Check-in on their relationships at work
    - o Ask if they feel safe to ask others for help
    - o Ask if they feel comfortable sharing mistakes
    - o Help them connect to the right team members
- ☐ Ask if there is anything they are hearing from colleagues that puzzles or concerns them
- ☐ Ask what else they would like to talk about
- ☐ Summarize your action items to support them and ask if you missed anything.
- ☐ Thank them and share your interest in talking next week

Clear communication, especially about the "WHY" behind changes, is critical for buy-in and alignment. In fact, a lack of clear and prompt communication about why changes are happening leads to resistance, disengagement, poor implementation, and lower morale.

Respectful Communications are also key. Christine Porath studies the effect of workplace incivility on people. Rudeness, disrespect, mocking, offensive jokes all fall into the incivility bucket. She discovered incivility affects the target and all witnesses! **80%** who experienced incivility on the job worried about it later distracting them from their work, **66%** reduced their work efforts, and **12%** left the organization! Cisco heard these numbers and estimated they lose at least **$12 million** each year due to incivility at their workplaces. To understand why costly incivility persists, take 15 minutes to watch Christine's TedTalk listed in our references.

14 Key Workplace Communication Statistics

How is the working world communicating today and what is it costing organizations globally? Here are crucial statistics on **WHY** Communication matters:

- **86% of employees** cite the lack of effective collaboration and communication as the main causes for workplace failures.
- **97%** of employees believe communication impacts their task efficacy on a daily basis.
- Communications barriers could be costing businesses around **$37 billion** a year.
- **16% of managers prefer** email interactions to avoid feeling awkward or uncomfortable in verbal communications.
- Poor communication is affecting trust for **45% of workers**
- When employees are offered better communication technology and skills, productivity can increase by **up to 30%**.

Introduction

- **28% of employees** cite poor communication as the reason for not being able to deliver work on time.
- Organizations with connected employees show productivity increases of **20-25%**.
- **64% of businesses** list communicating their 'strategy, values, and purpose' to employees as a key priority.
- **86% of corporate executives,** educators, and employees cite ineffective communication and poor collaboration as reasons for failures in the workplace.
- Employees who feel their voice is heard in the workplace are almost five times **more likely (4.6x) to feel empowered** to deliver their best work.
- **39% of employees around the world** feel that people don't collaborate enough within their organization, yet
- **75% of employers** rate collaboration and teamwork as 'very important'.
- Miscommunication costs companies with 100 employees an average of **$420,000 per year**.

Key Outcome: Great communication fuels success in any workplace. It's how we get stuff right and get stuff done (GSD), build awesome collaborative teams, and make meaningful, aligned progress.

So, how can you become a master at this? Let's take proven ideas and apply them with a fresh, real-world spin.

How to Model Communication

As with any practice or change, your teams take their cues from you. If you talk about the importance of rich and thoughtful communication and don't take the time to do it, neither will they.

Walk the Talk, Don't Just Talk the Talk

- Lead by Example:

    How YOU communicate sets the standard.

    - Do you give updates promptly?
    - Do you say why their work makes a difference?
    - Do you actively listen to concerns?
    - Do you celebrate WINs publicly?
    - Do you give praise frequently, even for small wins?

    Employees notice everything, so model the behavior you want to see.

- Make it Visible:

    If "open communication" is your goal, be transparent about your process. Share meeting notes widely, recap town halls in bullet points, and show that hiding info isn't the norm.

    Use Worksheet C3 to discover if your teams think your organization is transparent in their communications. Are there improvements you want to recommend?

Do you want to find out what other managers are hearing from their employees? Encourage them to use Worksheet C3 too. Find a constructive way to share the rich feedback upward.

Create Conversation Spaces

- Informal Wins:
  Not everything needs an agenda. Coffee breaks and team lunches—encourage these without hovering. Sometimes, the BEST feedback happens "off the record," fostering that relaxed trust.

- Ask, THEN Tell:
  Town hall Q&A time shouldn't be an afterthought. Prioritize hearing everyone's concerns first! Your announcements will have a much greater impact if your team just told you what they need to hear and you can tailor your updates to meet those needs.

Match the Message to the Person

- Some people crave details, others want the big picture.
- Some people LOVE meetings, others dread them.
- Hold meetings when it makes sense for your message: send a quick email when that's better.
- Explore what suits your team (quick surveys work!) and offer options:
  - 1:1 chat
  - Email updates
  - In person

- On a call or virtual
- Continuously adapt to how your team members like to receive information.

Use Worksheet C1 to take a communication preference audit with your teams. Participation increases dramatically when the format isn't forced.

Create Communication LOOPs

- Normalize Regular Check-Ins:

    Use the checklist (on page 26) at the start of this section and evolve it as you go. Check-ins don't have to be long, but they do have to be frequent. Ask team members, "What's ONE thing about our communication that is working well? ONE thing that needs improvement?" Use what you learn and add it to your checklist.

- "You Matter" Moments:

    Thanking people for a specific email or thoughtful question reinforces good habits. These tiny efforts fuel a genuinely appreciative, communicative workplace.

Grow Authentic Connections:

- **The Personal Touch**
    - Make a list of key colleagues/contacts.
    - Next to their name, add ONE non-work thing you know about them, even if it's small.

- During your next chat, reference it casually: "Isn't your son's baseball game this weekend?"

That tiny bit of effort shows you pay attention to them as a person.

- **Find Your Overlap: Pave the Way Forward**
    - Before brainstorming on a new project, ask collaborators: "What's your IDEAL outcome here, apart from just delivering results?"
    - Their answers reveal where your goals naturally align
    - This makes "selling" your ideas much smoother later.

Empower Mid-Level Management: Their buy-in will make or break employee engagement. Support them in replicating your good habits with their teams and encouraging them to replicate them. Your train-the-trainer model builds engagement in the most efficient way. You don't need to micromanage the whole process.

Model the Behavior: People learn more from how you handle yourself than from any abstract advice. Stay composed in tense moments, and show empathy even with prickly colleagues – this sets the tone for your whole team.

Body Language 101: Be aware of your posture, facial expressions, and other subtle cues. Make sure your nonverbal cues don't accidentally undermine your message.

Know Your Limits: Some situations may require outside help (A Coach, HR, trained mediator). Admitting this isn't weakness, it's being responsible.

Introduction

How to Coach Communication Practices

We hope the last section inspired you to model effective communications to engage your people at work. Let's now address how you can coach them to practice and hone new skills in their own communications. To optimize employee engagement, everyone needs to practice top-notch communication skills.

From our experiences working with hundreds of managers and thousands of their team members, we can safely say they will need your help to become better communicators. Processing and collaborating with others on what we hear and say is how humans excel—and where AI can't keep up. You can help your teams be future-ready for the new workplace, where collaboration and constructive feedback—the soft skills—trump the hard skills like coding and testing, where AI excels.

Coach the "Soft Stuff" Because, Guess What, It's HARD

- Skills Workshops:

    Assume most folks weren't trained in good feedback, tough conversations, etc. These aren't magically acquired! Invite a pro (internal or external) to lead skills workshops. Make it fun and offer follow-up.

Role-Playing is Your Best Friend . . .

. . . and it will be fun, especially if you volunteer in the first role play! Awkward conversations feel much LESS scary when rehearsed. Take advantage of team meetings to practice delivering difficult feedback or responding to tricky scenarios.

Bring real life incidents from your experience into the role-plays. Then rehearse and practice how to handle that disgruntled client or navigate a disagreement. It will probably feel silly at first . . . watch as it lessens their fear and builds your teams confidence in their ability to communicate with empathy. They will thank you the next time they are able to prevent expensive real-world mishaps using their new skills.

Try Worksheet C5 to Practice Role-Playing Scenarios.

- **Go Beyond "Not Avoiding:"**

It's not just that *avoiding* tough conversations is harmful, it's that actively pursuing the tough conversations builds emotional resilience within your team. The goal is to normalize those difficult situations, reduce the fear factor, and reframe them as opportunities for growth as we practice how we handle them.

- **Finding that Common Ground with individuals/groups:**

This isn't always easy. So, let's start small:

- What do you BOTH or ALL ultimately want?
    - a successful project?
    - a happy customer?
    - an aligned team?

Reminding each other of that shared goal can create a starting point for collaboration.

- **Validate the 'Other Side':**

  Acknowledge opposing views before launching into your pitch. Starting with, "I know everyone loves the old format, AND it's familiar...but has it kept up with our growth?", may diffuse their resistance to your idea.

  As passionate humans, we often focus on having our own viewpoints understood. Validating the other person's feelings first is usually better. Is there knowledge you lack that explains their actions? Try mirroring: "I hear you're feeling frustrated/under pressure/etc." to lessen defensiveness upfront.

Genuine curiosity helps you avoid assumptions.

- **"How are they feeling?" Isn't Just Emotional:**

  Sometimes, physical factors play a role – perhaps someone is tired, overwhelmed, hungry... even the color in the room is precipitating their reactions.

  Ask genuinely open-ended questions: "It sounds like there's a lot going on...can you fill me in?"

- **Expressing Yourself is ALSO About Listening:**

  Yes, how you SAY things matters, but equally important is how you hear the other person's response. Do they feel truly heard? Ask clarifying questions to ensure you're not rushing to offer a solution before fully understanding the concern.

Try Worksheet C4 to understand how important being heard is and how easily it is derailed! Most of your team will remember the whispering game from their childhoods. You may hear even more laughter among adults!

- **Trust Requires Action:**

    Just *hearing* someone doesn't magically solve problems. If a colleague opens up about a workload issue, is there something you can ACTUALLY do to help? If not, be honest and transparent about that. Small, consistent actions create more trust than big promises and no action.

Acknowledge 'Loud' AND 'Quiet' Voices:

How can you coach teams to make sure they hear from those who are less vocal? Here is an example we see a lot with our clients: Not everyone thrives in brainstorming sessions where everyone shares ideas out loud as soon as the root cause is identified. We suggest using the first 3-5 minutes of the brainstorming session for quiet individual reflection when everyone writes their suggestions on sticky notes or in their notebook. When time is up, everyone shares and discusses their suggestions. This simple pause is often all it takes to highlight the ideas from the quieter voices as well as from the louder ones.

It's all about creating alternate paths for input such as:

- An anonymous suggestion box

- After-meeting written critiques

Valuable ideas come from everywhere. Let's make sure we create situations to hear from everyone on the extrovert to introvert scale. Otherwise, half of our best ideas may never be heard.

Try Worksheet C6 to practice ways to include all voices in the conversation.

How to Reward Communication

- **Belonging Matters:**

  We are social animals. Feeling part of a team creating positive change is often its own reward. Frequently remind people how their skills play into the bigger picture. Tell them you believe in their contributions.

- **Support Systems Work Both Ways:**

  Offering praise and helping out when you can isn't a one-way street. Being a champion for your colleagues not only earns respect but helps you understand their perspectives and needs.

- **Reward the Quieter for Being Less Quiet:**

  Did a usually quieter team member offer suggestions in the last problem solving session? Acknowledge them privately in your next check-in and ask for their permission to acknowledge them publicly at the next team meeting.

- **Reward the Louder for Being Less Loud:**

    Did a usually louder team member spend more time listening than talking in the last team meeting? Same reward as above: Acknowledge them privately in your next check-in and ask for their permission to acknowledge them publicly at the next team meeting.

- **Reward a Successfully Navigated Confrontation:**

    Ask a team member who was in the room to share what they saw and heard. Did the facilitator validate the other sides' concerns? Did they deescalate the confrontation? Reward specific gains!

- **Reward a Successful Client Negotiation:**

    Did a team member negotiate successfully with a notoriously difficult client or a new client? Ask another team member to share what they saw.

Tip: Peer to peer recognition is often the best reward!

How to Celebrate Communication

- **Celebrate Micro-Successes:**

    A particularly productive project thanks to better communication? Big it up! Show the tangible result of this work... that's more convincing than 100 memos. Reminder: No one is expected to become a dazzling communicator overnight! Celebrate small successes as your teams incorporate new communication skills into their way of working!

- **Track Your Successes:**

    - Did your team use a story during a demo or presentation to engage the audience? Write it down and publicly celebrate this success at the next all-team meeting. The more positive results you celebrate, the more these techniques will take hold on your teams.

    - Did your team ask for feedback from you and the team after their last demo? Celebrate this as a huge win to step up their communication game. Make sure you offer constructive feedback to reward the effort. "You convinced me you are passionate about your solution and answered questions clearly. I captured your answers in our customer feedback log. Let's make sure we revisit this feedback in the next demo. Speaking of which, have you thought about using our systems team to integrate with Team C at the next demo? "

Introduction

How to Sustain Communication

It's an Ongoing Journey: Communication trends and needs evolve just like anything in organizations. Stay current on effective practices, and always be willing to admit what ISN'T working and ask for their input when you share your initial plans to fix it.

Genuineness is Key:

Forced interest never fools anyone. Start by finding points of genuine connection. Maybe it's a shared hobby, a similar work challenge, whatever. Small talk matters when it's sincere.

Ask (and Actually Listen): The Art of Listening

Ask a question, then let the answer hang in the air. People often keep talking and reveal valuable info. Summarize what you hear to avoid misunderstandings, it shows you care.

Questions reveal what motivates people. "What's the biggest challenge on your project right now?" is infinitely more powerful than generic pleasantries. Remember what you learn – their answers matter later!

When you ask for feedback, ask for specific tips on how to improve. When you give feedback, avoid generalizations – talk about what worked, what didn't, and ways to get better.

Try Worksheet C2 to practice active listening with your teams. It's great for team-building too!

Introduction

Become a Storyteller: Make Your Message Memorable

Facts Bore, Stories Stick: Data is necessary, but people remember how you made them *feel*.

- Did a past failure lead to a good solution? Weave it in.
- A client testimonial with a happy ending is worth more than bullet points.
- For your next presentation, replace your usual intro with a mini-story hook: "Remember that time we lost client X to bad communication? Good news, that won't happen again...". It instantly sets the stage. They will remember you better without the usual introduction of who you are! In fact, they will be asking, who is that again?
- Find *one* surprising stat to use as the headline in your story about new sales data. "Our sales dropped 10%...but here's where we CRUSHED our competitors anyway." This engages curiosity, so the audience wants more details. They have a context for your data and may even stay awake and ask questions.

The Anatomy of a Good Story: It doesn't require dragons: A simple "struggle leading to a transformation" structure has its own power. "Remember how process X used to be? I heard your woes. My idea can finally fix that..." creates engagement right away.

Tap Into the Familiar: Relate abstract concepts to what your team already knows. Analogy is your friend: "This project is like our successful Y launch, but..." helps avoid that glazed-over look.

Surprise and Humor Win: Unexpected elements wake people up. A funny, relevant anecdote (be sure it's in good taste!), or a twist in your presentation keeps things fresh, which translates to your idea feeling "fresh" as well.

Persuasion with a Purpose: Motivating Action

Secrecy's Power (and Danger): Humans are curious creatures. Hinting at "insider info" draws attention, as long as you can deliver. Secrecy about insider info works best for early-stage concepts. Trust is shot if your "insider info" turns out to be concrete plans they will hear about tomorrow.

"Let Them Have the Aha Moment:" Instead of telling someone why they SHOULD support your idea, frame it as an open question: "How might implementing X lead to faster turnaround times in YOUR department?" Guide them to discover the answer themselves; this wins people over every time.

Exclusivity Works...Selectively: Creating a sense of being part of something special motivates. This may be access to a pilot project or an exclusive vote of confidence. Beware of broad promises that make it harder to maintain that special feeling. Keep the context narrow and the duration short.

Expertise Builds Trust: Showing, not just claiming, that you're knowledgeable inspires faith. Share stories about relevant past successes or highlight your research. Add humility by sharing a few failures too. People believe someone who knows their stuff and who has learned from past successes and failures.

How to Rescue Failing Communication

Criticism Comes in Disguises:

Complaining about external things ("This client is terrible!"), gossip, even excessive sarcasm can erode trust. It's not that negativity is banned; it's just that being solution-oriented goes further than dwelling on problems.

Win-Win, Not Conquest:

"Why is MY idea the best?" is the wrong mindset. Find the overlap: how does your idea solve THEIR problem, make THEIR job easier, further THEIR goals? When the 'win' is shared, getting buy-in is easy.

It doesn't mean you AGREE; it means you see them as human.

Honesty vs "Being a Jerk":

Being direct requires tact, not brutality. Focus on impact over intent. For example:

"Your tone is coming off as condescending" is honest and solution-focused.

"You're acting like an idiot" is neither honest nor helpful. It shames the other and makes you look like the idiot.

Timing is Key:

Sometimes, taking a break is THE most proactive thing you can do. Reassure the person or group that you'll revisit the discussion in a set time (a few hours, the next day) when everyone is calmer.

Empathy is Everything: Get into their shoes!

Curiosity as a Toolkit: Be genuinely curious about actions you are seeing and words you are hearing. Think to yourself:

"What's driving this reaction?"

Is this a pattern with this person?

Is this a temporary stress response?

By putting yourself in their shoes, you can frame your response to the situation rather than react without empathy for the other person.

Tailor Your Approach:

What works for outgoing Susan won't work for quieter Mike. The principles remain the same, but how you communicate these should reflect your leadership strengths.

Don't Fake It:

People have super strong sensors to detect inauthentic behavior. If you can't find a way to be enthusiastic about their idea honestly, maybe that idea needs tweaking! Everyone and the idea will benefit from authentic, constructive feedback rather than faked enthusiasm,

Ethics ABOVE Tactics:

Being manipulative may work in the short term, but it always destroys trust in the long term. Using techniques to silence dissent or shame someone into changing sides will destroy trust and ruin any shot at true engagement.

The Never-ending Journey

Spoiler alert: you'll never reach communication perfection. It's about continuously learning and being humble enough to try new approaches. Great communication is how engaging connections and positive changes happen.

Start using these tips and watch how your work (and work life) transforms! Reach out and let us know what you are learning. We are always thrilled to engage with you!

 Grab Your Compass!

 Hit The Pause Button!

Worksheets

COMMUNICATION

Worksheet C1: The Communication Audit

Objective:

To identify gaps, bottlenecks, or misalignments in existing communication channels and methods.

Materials Needed:

- Paper and pen
- Whiteboard (optional)
- Sticky notes (optional)

Steps:

1. **Identify Channels**: List all the communication channels used within the team or organization. This could include email, Slack, meetings, etc.
2. **Rate Effectiveness**: On a scale of 1-5, rate the effectiveness of each channel.
3. **Collect Feedback**: Gather feedback from team members on what works and what doesn't for each channel.
4. **Identify Gaps**: Note any missing channels or areas where communication could be improved.
5. **Action Plan**: Create a plan to address the gaps and improve existing channels.

Reflection:

Take a moment to discuss the findings and plans for implementation with the team.

Worksheet C2: The Listening Circle

Objective:

To improve active listening skills among team members.

Materials Needed:

- A quiet room
- Timer

Steps:

1. **Set Up**: Team members sit in a circle. One person starts by speaking on a given topic.
2. **Time Limit**: The speaker has 2 minutes to speak without interruption.
3. **Active Listening**: The rest of the team actively listens, without preparing a response.
4. **Rotate**: After the speaker finishes, the person to their left summarizes what was said before speaking on the topic themselves.
5. **Continue**: Continue rotating until everyone has spoken and listened.

Reflection:

Discuss the experience. Was it difficult to listen without preparing a response? Did anyone learn something new about their colleagues?

Worksheet C3: Transparency Workshop

Objective:

To foster an environment where employees feel comfortable sharing information openly.

Materials Needed:

- Paper and pen
- Flipchart or whiteboard

Steps:

1. **List Concerns**: Team members anonymously write down concerns they have about transparency in the organization.
2. **Group Discussion**: Collect the concerns and discuss them openly as a group.
3. **Prioritize**: Rank the concerns by importance.
4. **Action Plan**: Develop strategies to address each concern and assign responsibilities for implementing these changes.

Reflection:

Reflect on how the team feels about the current state of transparency and the plans to improve it.

These exercises aim to break down communication barriers and create a more transparent, collaborative work environment. Regularly practicing these activities can lead to meaningful improvement in how your team communicates and, consequently, in overall employee engagement.

Introduction

Worksheet C4: Whispering Gallery

Objective:

Highlight how even well-intentioned communication can become distorted – this makes open discussions crucial to clarity.

Materials Needed: None

Steps:

1. **List Concerns:** Ask each team member to silently consider situations where important information may not have reached them or may have been unclear. They don't need to write these down.

2. **Group Discussion:** Choose a volunteer to share a simple fact (e.g., a customer name, a project deadline). In a circle, they whisper this fact to the next person, and so on until it reaches the final participant.

3. **Prioritize:** Did the initial message remain intact? Have the group discuss where miscommunication is likely to occur, focusing on process barriers rather than blaming individuals.

4. **Action Plan:** What systems could help (clearer emails, dedicated update meetings, etc.)? Brainstorm together, choosing 1-2 simple yet impactful changes to try.

Reflection:

How confident does the team feel about receiving the RIGHT info when they need it? What will success look like after implementing the action plan changes?

Worksheet C5: The Role-Play Challenge

Objective:

Understand the emotional impact of different communication styles, increasing empathy and promoting healthier dialogues.

Materials Needed: Paper and pen, pre-written scenarios

Steps:

1. **List Concerns:** Brainstorm common communication problems: vague feedback, dismissive comments, etc. Write 3-4 short scenarios from your context.

2. **Group Discussion:** In pairs, partners each pick a scenario. Assign them a delivery style (angry, enthusiastic, bored, etc.). They'll practice delivering the SAME lines with their assigned tone.

3. **Prioritize:** After each act-out, the group prioritizes which styles felt most productive/damaging and WHY. Focus on what works, not shaming anyone.

4. **Action Plan:** Can the team agree on ground rules for tough conversations? (e.g., focusing on solutions and acknowledging the other person's feelings).

Reflection:

Did this exercise change anyone's mind about how they deliver feedback? Can the team commit to trying healthier approaches even when stressed?

Worksheet C6: Inclusive Brainstorm

Objective:

Recognize the barriers some experience in group settings, prompting solutions that ensure everyone gets heard.

Steps:

1. **List Concerns:** Think about meeting experiences: Who's always talking? Whose ideas get dropped? Anonymously, write these patterns down.
2. **Group Discussion:** Share those concerns without name-calling to spark awareness. Ask, "What might those left out be feeling?"
3. **Prioritize:** During the discussion, prioritize psychological safety for each team member. We are going for accurate reflections with no judgment.
4. **Action Plan:** What steps can we take to improve participation? (e.g., time limits on one person talking, appointing someone to seek opinions from quieter members).

Reflection:

Does the team now recognize unconscious bias in collaboration? What would a truly inclusive meeting feel like?

Introduction

Case Study

When an Oil Giant Ditched the "That's Just the Way We Do Things" Attitude

Picture this: A major oil and gas company, all about big projects, strict rules, making big money. So far, so predictable. But what if they found out one thing was getting in the way of even MORE impressive results? Yep, turns out communication, or rather the lack of it, was the roadblock they weren't paying enough attention to.

Employee Feedback That Couldn't Be Ignored

Despite being good at their core business, surveys were saying "meh" in a big way. Employees felt out of the loop, ideas went nowhere (maybe right into the trash?), and that whole "teamwork" thing wasn't working so smoothly, especially on sites where you gotta know what the other guy's doing, like, YESTERDAY.

Leadership Finally Got the Memo...Change Was Needed

It's easy to blame "industry practices" for stuff like this, but this company's leadership woke up. They realized if they wanted to stay ahead in a field that's already kinda under pressure to evolve, the company culture itself HAD to change. More

Introduction

communication, less rigidity...sounded simple, but would it work?

The "Culture of Open Dialogue" Plan – Sounds Fancy, What'd They ACTUALLY Do?

1. Bigwigs Talked the Talk: It turns out execs in meetings all day aren't enough. They held open chats with folks at every level, sharing the "why" behind decisions, the kind of feedback most employees never receive.
2. Workshops Get Real: "Effective communication skills" sounds boring, but these focused on the messy parts – disagreements, giving feedback, making sure everyone actually understands the point before a critical task.
3. Breaking Down the Walls: Projects stopped being about who was in charge and more about getting the right mix of folks in the room. Turns out diverse teams clash a bit at first but get to better solutions faster when they're forced to talk it out.
4. Spill Your Gut, No Retaliation: Anonymous feedback isn't new, but they took it seriously. Town halls weren't just for announcements, they tackled those concerns on the spot. Took some guts, but showed those complaints WEREN'T going in the circular file.

So, Did Talking (The Right Way) Make Them Richer? Kinda...

They did this over a year, not some crazy overnight sprint. It was bumpy, but after 12 months, here's what changed:

- Employee Engagement JUMPED: 30% higher scores is no joke. People felt like they weren't just working *for* the company but *with* them.
- Safety AND Speed Improved: Teams who can communicate well wasted less time and had fewer "whoops" moments.
- "Dumb Idea" Might Be Genius: Employees now felt safe to pitch new stuff. This is gold for big, slow-moving industries trying to keep up with the greener, techier ways of doing things.

Bottom Line:

This case study shows that even 'old school' companies can change. It's not just about feel-good slogans. Talking openly, admitting when stuff's bad, and giving real feedback improved how that oil giant operates, from site safety to the fancy executive offices.

It's Not Too Late For You, Either

They started small but stayed consistent with coaching and guidance. It's an inspiration for other oil and gas folks, but honestly, ANY company where rigid mindsets or bad communication are a problem should take note.

Introduction

Lessons for Leadership

Ownership Over Culture:

It's easy to blame low engagement on employees themselves ("lazy millennials" etc.). This case study proves that effective leadership takes responsibility for shaping culture, not just hoping that it will fix itself.

Vulnerability vs. "Authority":

Execs admitting they don't always have the best answer or that past processes failed truly builds trust. People respect honesty over fake perfection they know isn't real.

Change Takes Time, and Constant Adjustment:

This wasn't a 30-day "fix." They phased things in, got feedback, adapted... treating communication change as a long game, not a quick win.

Symbolic Signals Matter:

It's not enough to change *actions; the* symbols also have to align. Execs holding talks in less fancy offices, using the same anonymous feedback forms as everyone else; these small cues build buy-in.

Communication Skills as Practical, Not "Soft"

Targeted Training:

"Effective communication" sounds bland. Tailoring workshops to the real problems (conflict, unclear instructions, etc.) keeps engagement high. People see immediate use for what they're learning.

Focus on Outcomes, Not Just Style:

The goal isn't for everyone to become a public speaker. Did "misunderstanding X" go down after training? Were project delays prevented? This data reinforces that learning to listen is as important as learning to present.

Not Everyone Learns the Same Way:

The company offered options, such as workshops, mentoring, and even informal support groups. Not everyone thrives in the same environment, making learning less of a hurdle.

Breaking Down Silos

Cross-Functionality is Mandatory, Not Optional:

Forcing diverse teams to work together highlights where rigid departmental thinking fails. People realize what the "finance people" actually do, etc., and that changes how they communicate day to day.

Celebrating the Awkward Phase:

Initially, throwing different personality types together CAN cause slowdowns. Leadership anticipating this, acknowledging it, and providing tools to handle conflict becomes vital in making this stage productive, not destructive.

Making Collaboration Easier = People Will Do It:

Tools matter! If employees hate your internal shared docs system, no amount of cheerleading will improve cross-team work. The ease of real-time feedback loops, etc., can be the make-or-break factor.

Feedback That Creates Actual Change

Transparency Isn't a One-Time Event:

The consistent use of open forums, town halls, etc., builds the expectation that voices matter. If those avenues feel performative, people disengage quickly.

Leadership Follow-Through is Mandatory:

Acting on feedback shows it's a process, not a box to check. Even explaining why some criticism CAN'T be acted on keeps that trust intact (if done honestly, not with excuses).

Small Wins Still Matter:

Maybe employees wanted a gym and can't have it. BUT fixing the annoying software glitch they all complained about is still a signal that their concerns are heard, and makes it more likely they'll contribute further feedback.

Additionally, Some Notes on "Oil and Gas Specific" Issues

This industry often uses language of 'toughness' as a positive:

That mentality hinders honest two-way dialogue. Reframing problems as shared goals, emphasizing how good communication contributes to the "hard skills" they value builds more buy-in.

Remote Operations:

Sites, refineries, etc. require even more emphasis on clear procedures communicated in accessible language. It's a safety issue as much as a culture one. This case study's success is highly compelling to comparable workplaces.

Communication Follow-up: If you have questions about how to apply the communication workshops or actions in your context, please reach out to us here:

LEARNING

Build a "Learn It All" Workplace

(Without Being Totally Annoying About It)

Why Is Learning Critical to Employee Engagement?

"Learning Organization" guru Peter Senge believes your **only** competitive advantage is your organization's ability to learn faster than the competition. And you know it is vital for your organization to stay competitive in today's rapidly changing marketplace. What will happen to your organization if your employees do not know how to use new tools and skills that are helping competitors become more productive? Today in 2024, a great example is AI!

- Studies show that organizations with strong learning cultures have a **30-50% higher retention rate** than those that don't. Employees often feel valued and are more loyal when employers invest in their development.
- A study by the National Center on the Educational Quality of the Workforce (EQW) found that a 10% increase in educational development produced an 8.6% gain in total productivity.
- IBM reported a 10% increase in workforce skills led to an $80,000 increase per person in the annual revenue of a company.
- A comprehensive Gallup study reveals that training based on a person's strengths is inextricably linked to overall employee engagement, achieving the following results:
  - **9 to 15%** increase in employee engagement
  - **8 to 18%** increase in employee performance
  - **14 to 29%** increase in profits

In *Drive*, Daniel Pink demonstrates that humans desire autonomy, mastery and purpose. A culture of continuous learning enables employees to choose their learning trajectory and master new competencies that align with the organization's purpose. This is integral for keeping employees! If they aren't learning, they'll leave!

In 2024, the average cost of replacing an employee is up to **2x the employee's annual salary**. Turnover is real and is impacting your bottom line!

Okay, so you don't want employees who clock in and out, rather you want people to expand what they can do constantly. That's not only smart for staying competitive, but it's exactly what keeps jobs from feeling boring and stale.

Building a learning organization is the way to stop watching your employees leave and start watching them excel.

Key Outcome - This Isn't About Micromanaging

The goal is for people to feel in control of how they grow with the company. Ask them what they "yearn to learn" and back them up! Become their learning mentor and advocate instead of dictating every tiny course they take. Create a lasting culture of continuous learning.

How to Model Lifelong Learning

Nobody will buy your "lifelong learning" spiel if you've stopped learning. Are you too busy to learn? What message does that send to other leaders, managers, and teams? Here are some ways to model learning to your teams:

Learn by Example:

- Enroll in that challenging course.
- Tackle a new skill with genuine curiosity.
- Share your new skills and what you learned from them.

Your actions will ignite a hunger for learning. It will also encourage everyone to share what they have learned. Soon everyone in your organization will be learning everyday!

Leadership Learning Demo: Explore a topic or skill you are keenly interested in. It could be a leadership training or becoming proficient in a software tool. Then:

- Publicly announce your new interest, why it is important to you, and what you are learning.
- Post new learnings weekly and link them to the purpose and mission of your organization.
- Schedule an AMA (Ask Me Anything) to answer questions about what you are learning and how it will benefit you in your role and the organization.

How to Coach Learning Practices

Ready to Build a Team That Actually *Wants* to Learn?

Picture a team of unstoppable knowledge fiends – hungry for growth, ready for whatever the world throws their way. You can infuse cutting-edge learning into your company's DNA and create a culture where your employees learn faster than the competition. Learning can be a secret weapon that catapults your company to the top.

Here's how you make it happen:

- **Ask First, Assign Later:** Instead of generic, top-down learning plans, find out what fires up the learning engine for your people. Is it mastering a new application? Or tackling a skill that will push their careers forward? When they have a say in their own development, it ignites motivation and engagement.

- **Variety is the Spice of Growth:** Let's be real; some online learning platforms are about as thrilling as watching paint dry. Spice it up! Get creative! Organize job shadowing opportunities, set up 'lunch and learn' knowledge swaps, or invest in sending high-potential folks to industry events that expand their minds.

Mentor Matchmaking: Pair up rookies with veterans for informal knowledge sharing and support. Make sure mentors are comfortable in their role to guide, answer questions, provide hands-on support. Create a simple form where people list skills

Learning

they want to learn or are confident teaching – then set up those pairings!

This taps into the expertise that already exists within your team, builds bonds, and accelerates learning organically.

New Hire Knowledge Hunt: Instead of giving new hires the corporate handbook, give them a scavenger hunt list of knowledge to find within their first two weeks. Include tasks like finding answers on the intranet, shadowing another team, or interviewing someone experienced. They will learn more by doing and love their first weeks on the job!

Ticking HR boxes is more about your career than their learning, and they know it. If you really care about their growth and development, you need to get personal with their learning goals.

Make learning a personal opportunity and a key to success - yours, theirs, and the company's. As their learning mentor, you can bring learning back to life.

How to Reward Learning

Create Knowledge-Sharing Rituals: Make exchanging ideas a natural part of your workplace. Schedule hackathons, encourage regular 'show and tell' sessions, or create an internal knowledge repository to showcase people's insights.

Skill-Swap Fridays: Block out the last hour of every Friday for "skill-swap sessions" when anyone gets to present their A Game – Excel tricks, project management systems, negotiation tactics – whatever benefits the group.

Make Learning Pass the Fit for Purpose Test: Those mandatory Friday workshops are a surefire way to kill morale, especially for anyone juggling responsibilities outside the office.

- Provide flexible options and learning formats that actually work for their schedules.
- Offer authentic 1 on 1 mentoring from qualified coaches and on-demand resources.
- Accessibility isn't just about being nice – it will deliver value for every single person, regardless of their circumstances.

LEARNING is Its Own REWARD! Carve out learning sprints and dedicate time each week for focused learning with no distractions. Block calendars, turn off notifications, and create a "deep work" zone. Even just one hour per week yields noticeable impact and gratitude.

How to Celebrate Learning

Celebrate Micro-Wins: Highlight those who put new skills into practice, not just final outcomes. Publicly congratulate that employee who finally nailed that tricky spreadsheet function or recognize the manager who tried a new coaching technique after training. Show that even small efforts count.

Celebrate Learning Like You Celebrate Sales:

Hitting those targets is essential, but so is recognizing progress. Highlight individuals who fearlessly step outside their comfort zone, publicly recognize those who complete certifications, and applaud teams who share their knowledge. Create a buzz around learning that reinforces its value.

Failure Spotlight: Turn screw-ups into a celebrated learning process. Hold monthly meetings where one team shares a significant misstep, analyzes what went wrong, and brainstorms how to avoid the same trap in the future. Show that failure is feedback, not shameful or embarrassing. We will revisit this later in the Reflection chapter.

Conference Debriefs: Don't just send people to events and call it a day. Require those who attend to give mini-presentations on their key takeaways and how they'll implement what they learned. Celebrate the takeaways and spread knowledge to others to maximize the return on learning investments.

The Problem-Solving Board: Create a dedicated space (physical or online) where teams can list challenges and bottlenecks they're stuck on. Encourage everyone to offer potential solutions, resources, or connections that might help. When a problem is solved, move it to WINS. Celebrate the WINS publicly!

How to Sustain Learning

Tie Learning to Real Outcomes: No one wants to feel like learning is just busywork. Clearly demonstrate how skill development ties to business goals, individual roles, and solving real-world problems. When people see the impact of their efforts, learning becomes truly meaningful.

Make Time and Space for Growth:

Learning shouldn't be something people squeeze in after hours when they're exhausted. Set aside dedicated time during work hours for skill development, knowledge sharing, or attending conferences. Show that learning is an investment, not just an afterthought.

Tips and Tricks to Sustain Learning

Flashcards and boring textbooks are outdated. Here are some proven, practical ways to sharpen and sustain learning based on the newest research in brain science and how humans learn.

Pocket Guides: Don't rely on your memory when juggling new skills. Craft short "cheat sheets" with key concepts, formulas, or step-by-step instructions you can keep at your desk or save on your phone for quick reference.

Mind Maps: Get those thoughts organized! Mind maps let you visualize complex ideas, brainstorm connections, and see the big picture at a glance. Throw out the sticky notes and create visual roadmaps instead.

Find Your Learning Crew: Humans aren't meant to always learn alone. Help your employees link up with colleagues who are interested in the same topics and turn learning into a social activity. They can swap insights, troubleshoot problems together, and hold each other accountable.

The 5-Minute Rule: Are spare moments wasted doomscrolling? Ask for suggestions for quick video tutorials, article snippets, or technique drills from the teams. Build a library and make it accessible so everyone can use it and update. Keep an eye on the updates and highlight new entries. Tiny, consistent learning efforts have a way of stacking up into major wins.

Teach to Learn: Want to truly test your understanding? Explain a concept to someone less experienced. Teaching back not only exposes gaps in your knowledge but also solidifies your grasp of the topic.

The Pomodoro Method: Feeling overwhelmed? Try the Pomodoro Technique – focused work sprints of 25 minutes followed by short breaks. These bursts of concentrated effort with built-in recovery can work wonders for productivity and keep burnout at bay.

Learning from Failure: No shame in messing up! Instead of focusing on errors, analyze why things went sideways. Turn each misfire into a lesson by asking: What could I have done differently? What resources or knowledge did I lack? What does this teach me for the next attempt? Embrace productive failing – that's where real growth hides. We'll talk more about this in our last section of CLOVER, Reflection.

Spaced Repetition: Try this technique first yourself. Use a spaced repetition system (software like Anki, or old-school flashcards) for memorizing key terms, techniques, or formulas. Repeat information at increasing intervals to lock it into your long-term memory. Did it work for you? Teach it back to your teams as a cutting edge option to cramming before a big demo or presentation.

Active Learning > Passive Listening: Active learning lets you and your teams apply what you're learning immediately. If it's a coding tutorial, you will write some code. If it's a sales talk, you will practice the technique on a colleague. We now know active engagement with content beats passively absorbing it. Coach your teams to avoid endless webinars and sit-and-listen trainings.

Reflective Breaks: Coach your teams to take short breaks after new concepts are introduced. Take a walk, jot down key takeaways, or talk through your understanding with a colleague to let the information sink in. Avoid powering through content mindlessly.

The Power of "How?": When learning something new, coach your teams to push beyond the "what" or "why" questions. Ask "How can I implement this?" "How does this apply to my current project?" This practical-focused mindset turns theories into tangible action.

How to Rescue Learning

Kill the Stigma of 'Not Knowing':

Create a space where asking questions is celebrated, not shamed. Encourage people to admit when they're stuck or confused. Normalize saying "I don't know, but I want to find out" as a sign of strength, not incompetence.

Stop Boring Them, Start Inspiring Them

Trainings should be fun, inspiring, and unleash real learning! Can we stop asking employees to view mandatory corporate videos and snooze seminars?

In recent years, the possibilities for interactive and engaging online learning have skyrocketed! These offerings are based on brain research about how people learn and retain knowledge. Guess what? Learning has to be engaging and relevant to be absorbed and retained.

Learning

Invest in workshops that inspire, bring in speakers who shake things up, and support employee-led initiatives to share knowledge with each other.

Turn Performance Feedback into Development Fuel:

What if performance reviews could provide frequent and relevant feedback to inspire employees to improve - They can!

Many organizations have stopped the dreaded annual performance reviews in favor of frequent, constructive, and actionable feedback sessions. Managers provide real support in real time. They help people tackle the areas where they need growth iteratively throughout the year. Weekly check-ins are less about judgement and more about inspiration where the opportunities to improve are endless!

Here is a way to add learning as a key topic during your weekly check-ins:

The "What Did You Learn" Review: Include a tailored section on what new skills they acquired, how they applied them, and what new areas they want to explore next. Make frequent engaged learning an active part of your partnership.

This is just a starting point to help you weave learning into the fabric of how you and your teamwork. Keep your learning practice fresh by experimenting to discover what works best for *your* team.

Learning

 Grab Your Compass!

 Hit The Pause Button!

We would love to hear how your learning practice is going and what you found helpful in your organization. Connect with us! We want to learn from you!

The worksheets mentioned in this section follow. Happy Learning!

Worksheet L1: Skill Inventory

Objective:

To identify the current skill sets within the team and recognize areas for development.

Materials Needed:

- Spreadsheet or paper and pen
- Whiteboard (optional)

Steps:

1. **Skill Listing**: Each team member lists their primary and secondary skills.
2. **Rate Proficiency**: Rate each skill on a scale of 1-5 in terms of proficiency.
3. **Identify Gaps**: As a group, identify any skill gaps that need to be filled.
4. **Learning Goals**: Set individual or team-based learning goals to fill the gaps.

Reflection:

Discuss the skill gaps and learning goals. Plan for regular check-ins to track progress.

Learning

Worksheet L2: Peer-to-Peer Learning Sessions

Objective:

To leverage internal expertise for mutual growth and skill development.

Materials Needed:

- Presentation equipment (laptop, projector)
- Note-taking materials

Steps:

1. **Topic Selection**: Team members propose topics they are knowledgeable about and would like to share.
2. **Schedule**: Create a schedule for peer-led learning sessions.
3. **Prepare**: The selected team member prepares a short presentation or workshop.
4. **Session**: Conduct the learning session, allowing time for questions and discussion.

Reflection:

What new skills or insights have you gained? How can this new knowledge be applied in your current projects?

Worksheet L3: Learning Journal

Objective:

To encourage reflective practice and continuous learning.

Materials Needed:

- Journal or digital notepad

Steps:

1. **Daily Recap**: At the end of each day, take 5-10 minutes to jot down what you learned, both in terms of technical skills and interpersonal dynamics.

2. **Weekly Review**: Once a week, review your notes and identify patterns or areas for improvement.

3. **Share Insights**: During team meetings, allow time for team members to share insights from their learning journals.

Reflection:

Discuss the value of keeping a learning journal. Have you identified areas for improvement that you might not have noticed otherwise?

These exercises are geared to foster a learning culture that can keep team members engaged, continually growing, and contributing at their highest potential. They should not be one-time activities but should be integrated into the regular rhythm of your team's operations for maximum effectiveness.

Learning

Case Study

Company: Let's call them "Odyssey Excursions"

- **The Challenge:** Odyssey Excursions was stuck in a training time warp. Generic videos on safety regulations, endless customer service webinars...employees' eyes glazed over faster than a week-old pastry. Meanwhile, guides lacked in-depth knowledge about destinations, sales teams needed better pitch techniques to sell those luxury upgrades, and a wave of new tech was leaving some veteran staff frustrated. Low morale and lost opportunities were starting to stack up.

- **The 'Aha!' Moment:** They realized – to thrive in a constantly evolving travel market, everyone needed to see learning as an ongoing journey, not a one-time, suffer-through-it event. Odyssey knew it had to create a culture where seeking new knowledge was exciting, engaging, and actually tailored to the unique challenges of their teams.

- **The Plan of Attack:**
    - **Ditch the One-Size-Fits-None Approach:** Generic training went out the window. They surveyed specific skills gaps for each department, from historical facts for tour guides to social media skills for marketing. This made learning targeted and immediately relevant.

- **Adventure-Themed Learning:** They branded their whole approach "Expedition: Upskill!" with themed badges, a progress tracker, and leaderboards. A playful spirit tapped into the company's love of exploration.
- **Mix It Up:** They ditched the lecture hall vibe. Job shadowing between veteran and rookie guides, destination "crash courses" led by locals, even travel video editing contests added fun to skill development.
- **Learning Rewards Beyond "Certificate of Completion":** Top learners in each area were given chances to be the first to test new tours, lead the development of educational resources for clients, or attend travel industry events

- The Results Odyssey Saw:
  - **Guides Went from Reciters to Experts:** Deeper knowledge meant more fascinating tours, higher client ratings, and even increased tips. Those historical fact sheets turned into captivating, customer-delighting moments.
  - **Sales Soared:** The team wasn't just pushing trips, they were advisors. Understanding what truly made destinations unique unlocked opportunities to suggest custom itineraries and those profitable high-end experiences.
  - **Tech Headaches Vanished:** Tech-resistant staff weren't left behind but partnered with tech-savvy colleagues. Knowledge went both ways! – seasoned

workers got digital help while teaching valuable industry insights.

- **Talent Magnet:** Word got out that Odyssey was the place for ongoing growth. They started attracting ambitious candidates and reduced employee churn rates.

Key Takeaway: In the travel business, passion and the thrill of constant 'upgrading' your knowledge is infectious. Odyssey wasn't just upskilling, they were crafting a company where learning itself was the ultimate destination. They showed that investing in people didn't just pay off – it powered thrilling growth they might never have achieved otherwise.

Learning

OPPORTUNITY

Why is Opportunity Critical to Employee Engagement?

Done right, **Opportunity** helps you forge a team that feels a burning ambition to grow alongside the company. They should not just see a runged ladder to climb but a dynamic rocket ready to launch! You want people fired up and ready to launch that next opportunity for the company and their careers.

- A 2022 report by LinkedIn Learning indicates that **94% of employees** say they would stay longer at a company if it invested in their career development.
- According to the Association for Talent Development (ATD), companies that offer comprehensive training programs have **218% higher income** per employee than companies without formalized training.
- These same companies enjoy a **24% higher profit margin** than those who spend less on training.

- A Survey by the Society for Human Resource Management (SHRM) found **only 29%** of employees are "very satisfied" with advancement opportunities available at their organization while **41% marked** advancement as "very important" to job satisfaction, engagement, motivation, and longevity.

KEY OUTCOME

Imagine your organization filled with people who aren't just content; they're thrilled to be on a path to meet their evolving personal and professional goals. They know each win fuels the next step in their journey. Their skills expand, and each opportunity for that next challenge separates your organization from the competition. Here, every team member feels valued. They see a future with your organization.

How to Model Opportunity Practices

When I talk to executives and leaders who have just gotten a promotion, I love to ask them, so what's your next move? You may be surprised to hear that on Day 1 of a new job; they almost always have their next move ready and waiting!

Your employees are no different.

In fact, are you already looking for that employee who can step into your job when you advance? Succession planning is the first step to modeling your aspirations for new opportunities. It also tags you as a smart leader who is proactively planning smooth transitions when you find that next opportunity.

"What Opportunities? I barely have time to do my actual job!"

Too often, growth opportunities remain obscure because they hide in a messy mix of internal communications, outdated documentation, or exist within the knowledge held by senior-level employees. Without intentional transparency, team members can quickly become disenchanted, assuming there is nowhere to move but out.

Here's how you can spotlight hidden opportunities for you and your teams.

Cultivate the Opportunity Mindset

- **Leaders Lead by Example:** Senior roles opening up? Don't default to external hires. Publicly encourage internal candidates – even those considered "long shots"

– to apply. Showcase your commitment to growing from within. See how to coach them to apply for new opportunities in **How to Coach Opportunity** – coming up next!

- **"I Made the Leap" Stories:** Highlight those who successfully shifted career trajectories within the company. Ask them to share how they prepared, the risks they took, and what support they received.

- **The '80% Rule':** Encourage a mindset of taking a reasonable "leap of faith." If someone with ambition has most, but not every required qualification, help them close the gap while on the job. Perfection over passion creates stagnation.

Additional Thoughts:

- **Mentorship Matters:** Connect hungry up-and-comers with more established professionals in other departments to bridge knowledge gaps and learn the internal 'language' of their desired field.

  See Worksheet OP4 to build mentorship opportunities at your organization.

- **Embrace Transparency:** If certain opportunities truly require external hires, be honest about why. Sharing these insights shows you respect internal talent and builds trust – and can help some ambitious minds identify future goals even if they aren't ready *today*.

Spotlight Those Hidden Opportunities

No more opportunities hidden in dusty manuals! Create a dedicated "Opportunity Hub" (physical or digital) AND keep it current! Update it in real time. Post stretch assignments, chances to shadow different teams, mentorship openings, ANYTHING that gets minds racing.

Create a Dedicated "Opportunity Hub"

- If HR is agile and engaged with your teams, you can partner with them to create this Hub. If not, create it yourself and make it visible to HR and other managers in your organization.
- **Make it Visually Engaging:** Think of it as a dynamic billboard broadcasting every chance imaginable! Make sure it is a stunning departure from that boring memo on the intranet. Here are some formats to consider:
    - **Physical Bulletin Board:** In a high-traffic area, create a space for pinned postings. Divide the board into categories like "Stretch Assignments," "Mentorship Openings," "Training Courses," in addition to new jobs. Use **BOLD** fonts and **pops** of color. Your goal is to **GRAB** attention!
    - **Virtual "Idea Marketplace":** Utilize a company-wide collaboration platform (like Slack or Notion) to gather opportunities in a streamlined space. Employees can subscribe to channels like "Skill Development" or "Project Teams Seeking Help" for targeted updates.

Opportunity

See Workshop OP3 to create an Internal Mobility Fair to learn about opportunities in different units within your organization.

- **Regular Spotlights:** Ensure nothing gets stale. Feature a specific opportunity on a rotating basis within company newsletters, presentations, even screensavers.

Beyond the Announcement: Provide "The Blueprint"

Don't leave people hanging with an opportunity title and a shrug. Each posting should include:

- **Skill Boost:** Be upfront about what learning this involves. New software? Specific leadership tactics? Clearly link every opportunity to tangible takeaways.

- **Why it Matters:** Spark that "oh, *I* could help with/do that!" Don't just say "open opportunity" – connect it to company goals, department-wide projects, or recurring issues everyone feels frustrated by.

- **The 'Apply' Process:** Remove mystery with crystal-clear steps. Who do they contact? Are there prerequisites? What timeframe are we talking about?

Bonus Moves:

- **Open Door Demo Sessions:** If the opportunity involves new technology or a change in process, don't assume everyone understands. Schedule quick "lunch and learn" sessions so your team can get "hands-on" and decide if it's a good fit.

- **'Success Stories' Spotlight:** If previous employees made significant growth by taking on these types of opportunities, share this story! Stories about how peers thrive are highly motivating.

How to Coach Opportunity Practices

Leaders and managers update and promote the **Opportunity Hub** for their teams, but it doesn't end there. Executives coach their leaders and leaders coach their managers to actively identify people who can be primed for those once hidden and now exposed gems on your **Opportunity Hub** (see last section).

Don't wait for self-motivated go-getters or even your next weekly check-in; proactively seek out your employees who might be eager to apply. Set up a chat today to offer suggestions about what you know or what you can learn together beyond what is posted.

Empowering your employees to seek out internal opportunities often reveals surprises! You may learn about previously unnoticed skills and experiences or become aware of training to help optimize their potential. Even if they don't take the new opportunity, you will both fine-tune your knowledge about their interests, skills, and gaps to help them seek a future opportunity.

Cultivate Talent Scouts, Not Gatekeepers

Forget about "you need X number of years experience for that." If someone sees an opportunity and has the gumption to step up, coach them to make their case. If you just let 'em try, you might be surprised who has the raw talent for something new.

The gatekeeping mindset kills potential and is the enemy of the team. Take note of rigid experience requirements, such as relying solely on "X years on the job." These stifle fresh talent and create a risk-averse culture where ambition doesn't pay off and existing employees get lost in the shuffle. Find those hidden gems on your teams and coach them to trust their own potential.

- **Shift Leadership Language:** Discourage managers or their employees from reflexively saying, "They're/I'm not ready yet." Instead, challenge them with, "What support would they/you need to succeed?" This flips the conversation to nurturing potential rather than dismissing ambition.

- **Focus on Transferable Skills:** Years spent in a "similar" role does not mean instant competence. Emphasize identifying the underlying skills needed for success. Can their work from various domains demonstrate critical thinking, adaptability, or the ability to thrive under pressure?

- **'Micro-Internships' as Auditions:** Don't throw someone in the deep end without support! Structure short-term experience opportunities to allow your eager beavers to contribute and prove themselves while minimizing risk. They get "field experience" within the desired area while building a track record that goes beyond their official resume.

- **Create the On-Ramp:** If there's an apparent skills gap between someone's ambition and the opportunity, build a ramp with them! Suggest skill-up courses, shadowing opportunities with experts, or mentorships to bridge the gap.

- **Case Studies Over CVs:** Ask candidates who lack "classic" experience to build a pitch for themselves. How would they approach the opportunity? What insights, unorthodox experiences, and personal strengths do they bring that others might not?

- **It Goes Beyond Individuals**
  - **The Blameless Retrospective:** Make retros standard practice for significant opportunity successes AND failures. Systems-level issues may be revealed, such as inefficient decision-making processes, resource gaps, etc. This isn't finger-pointing but uncovering how the company can become smarter about collectively looking at the 'body of evidence' when offering and rewarding opportunities.
  - **Highlighting the Course Correction:** Emphasize the pivot—what they changed mid-process when things weren't working. Adaptability is pure gold, even if the end goal couldn't be achieved initially.
  - **Let's be real: Crashes Hurt.** Demonstrate to your teams that a well-intentioned failure opens doors, not shuts them. Coach them to find the wonders a failure offers. Perhaps tell a story about one of your early failures that later fueled a win. You will boost their morale for the long term, and for the ambitious risk-taking, your organization needs!

Coach Growth Beyond Promotion:

Not everyone aims for the corner office. Craft career paths for your teams to show progression *within* specialties. Coach that master salesperson to get training on high-stakes deals or that brilliant designer to lead their own innovation projects. Make upskilling opportunities more important than new titles.

One Size Fits None = A Sure Way To Lose Great Talent

Assuming everyone wants to climb a traditional management ladder is short-sighted. Those who excel in their craft may crave respect and new challenges but not the headaches of leading others. Ambitious talent disengages when you only promote upwards, not *forward* with what sets their souls on fire!

This may be a great opportunity to find an HR partner who can help your organization encourage non-traditional career pathways with routes to more traditional roles.

Create "Expert Tracks" Alongside Management

- **The Skill Deep-Dive:** Offer specialized, high-value training exclusive to those hitting milestones within their focus areas. That expert salesperson doesn't get sent to generic leadership classes; they delve into negotiation tactics or closing million-dollar deals instead.
- **Project Power-Ups:** That amazing designer isn't just given more grunt work. Coach them to spearhead their own initiatives and prove their increasing leadership capabilities without managing people. Give them budgets, timelines, and cross-functional teams to work with – the challenge *is* skilling up.

- **Celebrate the 'Individual Contributor':** Make sure the growth of these experts is visibly recognized. Highlight their increasing expertise publicly, have them present company-wide, grant bonuses tied to measurable impact – even if their job title remains the same for now.
- **Don't Silo Their Brilliance:** As they become in-house gurus, leverage their expertise! Have them consult on other teams' projects, mentor less experienced peers, even contribute to setting product vision or marketing strategy. Cross-pollination is good for everyone's growth!

Craft Careful Inspiring Language Around "Expert Tracks"

Forget the "Alternative Path"; embrace the "Parallel Path." This shows these expert tracks have equal weight and importance within your company structure. See Worksheet OP2 to create growth pathways to fit each employee.

- **Visible Payoffs:** If you can, tie increasing seniority within these "expert tracks" to real perks. Consider access to special conferences, a small budget for self-driven research projects, or even dedicated sabbaticals to pursue side projects relevant to the company mission.
- **The 'Guru Council':** Involve senior-level experts (without managerial titles) in larger strategic discussions. It makes them visible as key players and ensures their insights aren't ignored simply because their focus isn't on direct reports.

How to Reward Opportunity Gains

Tap Into that Hidden Firepower

No matter their role, everyone has those little genius ideas swirling around their heads. Hackathons give those moments a place to become something awesome. Organize challenges focused on those nagging company problems everyone complains about, not some hypothetical crap no one actually cares to fix. Celebrate when WINs when the nagging problem disappears!

Prizes Are Cool, But Real Impact Is EVERYTHING Sure, some swag or gift cards are motivators. But what truly sets your company apart is showing everyone they're playing for keeps. Leadership gets hands-on with reviewing those winning ideas and commits to taking the best ones from concept to actual implementation! No more disappearing into the 'suggestion box' void. This fuels that burning belief that talent speaks loudest, regardless of someone's position on the org chart.

- **Risk-Taking = Visibility Boost:** Those who step up should get an audience. Maybe they present at an all-hands on what they learned. They might take the lead on brainstorming 'Plan B' solutions next time. The reward isn't just a bonus, it's increased influence and respect for their initiative.

- **Lead by Example:** Leaders need to admit when their 'big swings' failed too. Share a past fumble or that strategy call you totally miscalculated. Let your team see even at the top, playing it safe is the fastest way to become irrelevant.

How to Celebrate Opportunity Gains

- **Small Celebration Fund:** Managers have discretionary budgets for pizza parties after reaching a target. Let them use those same funds to reward 'good faith' fails by their team! It could be a post-flop lunch where the focus is on what they'll tackle differently next time.

- **The "Bravery Board":** Have a space where team members can (anonymously or not) brag about a recent stretch outside their comfort zone – big or small. It builds an internal culture of daring to think bigger!

You may recognize these bullets from an earlier section. Their importance bears repeating!

- **Celebrate the 'Individual Contributor' on the Parallel Expert Track:** Make sure the growth of these experts is visibly recognized. Highlight their increasing expertise publicly, have them present company-wide, grant bonuses tied to measurable impact – even if their job title remains the same for now.

- **The 'Guru Council':** As employees advance to in-house guru status, leverage their expertise! Have them consult on other teams' projects, mentor less experienced peers, even contribute to setting product vision or marketing strategy. Cross-pollination is good for everyone's growth!

Involve senior-level experts (without managerial titles) in larger strategic discussions. It makes them visible as key players and ensures their insights aren't ignored simply because their focus isn't on direct reports.

How to Sustain Opportunity Gains

"Where Do You Want to Be in 2 Years?" Conversations

Dreams without deadlines are daydreams! Ask forward thinking questions about career goals with near term milestones, like two years, in your regular check-ins with your employees – not every week but at least quarterly. Discuss, brainstorm, and write down specific ambitions with your employees. Take away action items bring your updates to your next meeting. Regular updates show you're serious about finding opportunities to make their dreams come true.

Generic conversations about 'career aspirations' during perfunctory performance reviews seem oh so hollow after doing it this way! Those past good intentions with no goals written down, no timelines discussed, and no follow-up evaporated quickly. Everyone on your team will see the difference between then and now. Now they know you can support their rise. Connect with us and let us know if this is working for you!

Ambition Roadmaps Create and Sustain Gains

See Worksheet OP1 to create ambition roadmaps with your teams.

- **Regular Check-ins, NOT Ritual Annual Reviews.** This is so important we touched on it earlier in our Communication Section and will revisit in Reflection too. Those dreaded yearly or even twice-yearly reviews just don't cut it.

Ask your leaders to mandate shorter but focused 'Goal Crafting' sessions with employees multiple times per year alongside weekly check-ins. This shows it's about actively aiding their journey, not ticking boxes.

- **Specific Destinations Populate a Roadmap:** Push back kindly on goals like "I wanna get better at leading." Help them articulate specific leadership skills on a specific opportunity they would like to spearhead. What does progress and success look like? You can help their dreams become achievable steps on a realistic ambition roadmap.

- **Document the Dream:** Help them write their very own clearly defined 'ambition roadmap' (even if it's just bullet points!). Coach them to outline their goal, specify needed resources, name a realistic timeline, and pinpoint where they need leadership support. You both sign this 'ambition roadmap'!

    See Worksheet OP1 to create 'ambition roadmaps' with your teams.

- **Revisit, Adapt, Conquer:** Weekly check-ins and follow-ups are non-negotiable. Use them to sustain progress on their 'ambition roadmap', discuss barriers, and adapt the roadmap as needed. Elevating your 'check-in' to active sustaining commitment to support them will sustain their hunger to exceed expectations.

- **Transparency Matters:** If not, every goal can be fulfilled, be honest about why. Did the company shift focus? Are resources tight? Take this opportunity to build trust by

Opportunity

explaining clear hurdles. Aim to leave their ambition intact.

- **Ambition Takes Many Forms:** Not everyone is management material. If someone aims to become a master coder or a recognized client negotiator, their roadmap reflects that specific skill growth. All paths take individual directions and align on sustained company success.

Link Every Opportunity to Purpose and Wellness:

- **Tie Every Opportunity Back to Purpose:** How does that training, or side project, contribute to your company's overall mission? Connecting those dots fuels sustained enthusiasm and demonstrates you're not just developing workers, but investing in individuals with goals that align to KPIs and the corporate mission.

- **Flexibility IS an Opportunity:** Let's be real – work-life balance matters more than ever. Remote options, flexible scheduling, support through transitions – this flexibility shows an actual investment in well-rounded folks. It attracts quality talent and sustains true loyalty in return.

How to Rescue Opportunity Losses

Risk-Taking Often Goes Unseen (Until Things Go South)

Are safe players still getting pats on the back on the back for hitting their numbers WHILE those who tried to slay internal dragons only get noticed when they fail? Rescue the bold risk-taking that sets great companies apart from the mediocre masses.

Rescue the Risk-Takers:

Spotlight those who took the leap, whether they succeeded wildly or failed gloriously. Public praise, small bonuses, and even the chance to share what they learned company-wide encourage initiative and show you have their backs.

Make Courage Contagious

- **Embrace the 'Epic Fail' Award:** Yeah, we're kinda serious. Hand out a light-hearted award at a company function for the risk that didn't quite pan out **yet** alongside your serious wins. This is a huge game-changer and a mindset shift to reward experiments. It will remove the fear of being sidelined when you go all out for a riskier win.

- **Spotlight Struggles Alongside Wins:** Do your project recaps focus only on flawless execution? Try highlighting the hurdles! Did a seemingly good idea crash? Was there a pivot midstream that salvaged the project? Normalize facing unknowns and watch the mindsets shift with you!

Opportunity

Make Failure a Launchpad: Not an Off-Ramp.

Did someone's reach exceed their grasp? Analyze *why* that opportunity flamed out. Was it bad timing, missing skills, or something else? Failing on ambitious experiments can open doors to future opportunities. Rescue your teams by coaching them to avoid letting it derail their career aspirations.

When setbacks are punished or met with a 'told you so' attitude, you crush risk-taking and breed a culture of fear and stagnation. People hunker down in their comfort zones, avoid innovation and limit possibilities to achieve great things. The costliest failures aren't those initial fumbles — it's when your team gives up trying entirely!

Here are suggestions on how to put aside the judges' gavel and pick up a magnifying glass to investigate a setback with your teams and rescue risk-taking and innovation that are so critical to the success of your organization.

- **Normalize "Productive" Failure:** Emphasize that the goal is progress, not bulletproof perfection. Create an organization-wide tagline around it. "Fail Fast, Learn Faster" may sound cliché, but it may catch on fast! Rescue that scrappy prototype from the "told you so" pile celebrate that it revealed a better angle.

- **Post-Crash Forensics:** Instead of the dreaded "post-mortem", reframe them as growth sessions. Focus on WHAT was learned, rather than assigning blame. Some guiding questions:
    - "Where was the disconnect between plan and outcome?"

- "What resources and/or people were missing that might have changed the equation?"
- "What did this reveal about how we typically operate?"
- "Were any aspects unexpectedly successful and worth taking forward?"

- **Knowledge Bank for Bravery:** Create a repository (anonymous if needed!) where anyone can share what they learned from failure – big or small. Treat it as the rescued treasure trove it is. This is especially good for remote teams – everyone needs to learn from the knowledge bank to avoid the same costly mistake!

- **Reframing, not "Soft Landing":** When someone's ambition has resulted in a flop, managers' language is everything. Don't just reassure them that everything will be fine. Focus on:
  - Specific strengths they demonstrated: Did they stay resourceful under pressure? Were they resilient when setbacks occurred? Rescue the value outcome even if the output wasn't ideal.
  - Rescue the Future with Actionable learning: Identify a skill to develop, a course to take, or a mentor who could bridge gaps in the future.
  - Rescue the ambition: Did they truly bite off more than they could chew? Could they take a slightly smaller step towards the same goal? Help them recalibrate to build momentum. Rescue their

ambition! It might be the one of the best things you do for their future with the organization.

Extra Fuel for the Flame

- **Diverse Teams Rescue:** Are team silos reforming? Try mixing engineers with marketing or tossing a seasoned leader in the ring with some newcomers. These unlikely combos generate amazing "ah-ha!" moments! Capture these moments in photographs and playbacks. No one will retreat to their silos once they have experienced the power of teams with diverse skills and experience.

- **Leadership Advocates Rescue:** Ask your leaders to circulate during a hackathon or team demo to hear ideas, give guidance, and offer encouragement. They can keep the buzz alive and approve resources for a great idea in the moment.

- **The Runner-up Rescue:** Funding and implementing every great idea is unrealistic. However, it's easy and impactful to dedicate time to share why second place wasn't funded. Take time to recognize cutting edge thinking even if funding or capacity isn't available now. Ask leaders to meet with the runner-up teams, to learn how to help them cross the line next time. The next big winner could emerge when runner-up teams learn what did or didn't resonate last time.

The Role of Prioritization & Purpose in Successfully Cultivating Opportunities

Understanding Prioritization

Prioritization within an organization is essential for aligning resources with the most impactful activities that support long-term strategic goals. It involves making informed decisions that balance immediate needs with future opportunities. Effective prioritization ensures that employees understand their roles within the broader context, which enhances engagement and productivity. By clearly defining what needs to be accomplished and aligning it with the organization's core objectives, employees are more likely to see the value in their work and stay motivated.

The Role of Purpose

Understanding the purpose of tasks and roles within an organization is crucial for deepening employee engagement. When individuals understand how their work contributes to the organization's goals, they experience a greater sense of belonging and significance. This connection not only boosts morale but also drives performance, as employees are more likely to invest in outcomes that resonate with their values and the larger organizational vision.

Integrating Prioritization and Purpose

1. **Strategic Alignment Workshops:** Conduct workshops to map out how individual roles and departmental goals align with the organization's strategic objectives. This helps employees see the bigger picture and

understand how their daily tasks contribute to larger goals.

2. **Clear Communication of Organizational Goals:** Regularly communicate the organization's strategic goals and progress towards them. This transparency helps to contextualize individual contributions and reinforces the significance of everyday tasks.

3. **Empowerment through Autonomy:** Encourage departments to identify and prioritize tasks that they believe will maximize their contribution to the organization's goals. This autonomy fosters innovation and ownership, enhancing engagement.

4. **Recognition Programs:** Develop recognition programs that highlight how individual contributions have furthered organizational goals. Recognizing these contributions can reinforce the importance of aligning personal achievements with business objectives.

5. **Feedback Loops:** Implement regular feedback loops where employees can express how their work aligns with the organization's purpose and suggest improvements. This feedback is invaluable for realigning efforts with organizational goals and employee expectations.

By focusing on these aspects, organizations can foster a culture where prioritization and purpose are at the forefront, enhancing employee engagement and driving success.

The Opportunity

By acting on these opportunity suggestions, activities and exercises, you can build an organization where employees feel they have the room and support to realize their ambitions at your organization. You will ultimately drive engagement and job satisfaction to new heights!

 Grab Your Compass!

 Hit The Pause Button!

Next up are four Opportunity Worksheets we referenced in the Opportunity sections. We hope you will use them and connect with us to offer your constructive feedback. Let's take this opportunity together!

Worksheets

Opportunity

Opportunity

Worksheet OP1: Roadmap to Personal Greatness

Section 1: The Fire Inside that Fuels your Ambition Roadmap

- NO to "Long-Term Career Goals"

- YES to "In 2 Years, I Will Be Known As The Person Who. . .": Ask them how they want to be seen and the kind of impact they crave.

- Follow-Up with "What gets you PUMPED about this ambition vision?": Make sure your vision cuts through vague ambitions and digs deeper to find the intrinsic motivation that fuels dreams.

Section 2: Powerful Moves on your Ambition Roadmap

- NO to "Areas for Improvement"

- YES to "My Superpowers": List 3-5 of your personal aces – those "WOW" things you do RIGHT NOW!

- Follow-Up with "The Missing Weapon": Identify 1-2 key skills that could take your work to the next level and help you realize your 'Fire Inside' goals.

Section 3: Ambition Roadmap Marks Realistic Opportunities

- NO to "Professional Development Opportunities"

- YES to "How I'll Grow Like a Boss": Here is space for the more traditional stuff like specific training, shadowing opportunities, special projects to contribute to, conferences that would supercharge your growth, etc.

- Now add "What obstacles do you and I foresee?": Coach them to be realistic, not just optimistic. Open up conversations about support systems they may need upfront.

Section 4: Ambition Roadmap Assistance

- NO to "Manager Comments"
- YES to "Leader's Role": Flip the script. Here leaders outline how they can directly support this goal: offer a chance to remove an obstacle, suggest specific opportunities, create stretch assignments, etc.

Bonus "Off the Roadmap" Areas

- Sometimes the goal seems so big it's overwhelming. Give space for visualizing it: Try a crude timeline drawing, a mind map, or anything that gets it out of their heads.

The Vibe We're Going For in the "Ambition Roadmap"

- Reach beyond the word document: Try a big sketchpad or a shared digital whiteboard. Find opportunities to tack on visuals and updates. Go for a living roadmap rather than a static plan.

- Honest Feedback is Essential: Ambition Roadmaps shouldn't be all sunshine and rainbows. Leaders need to be ready to gently challenge unrealistic fantasies and help focus ambitions for maximum impact in real time.

- Regular 'Ambition Plan Updates': Make notations on the roadmap at every follow-up. Note cleared and now new unexpected barriers. Ask if they are happy with the pace. Was their plan too modest – or too challenging? Then adjust as needed. Regular updates keep the ambitions and the roadmaps alive!

Worksheet OP2: Opportunity Mapping

Objective:

To identify existing and potential opportunities for career growth within the organization.

Materials Needed:

- Paper and pen
- Whiteboard (optional)
- Sticky notes (optional)

Steps:

1. **Current Roles**: List the existing roles within your team or organization.

2. **Career Paths**: For each role, identify potential career advancement paths.

3. **Skill Requirements**: List the skills or qualifications required for each advancement.

4. **Personal Goals**: Team members identify their own career aspirations.

5. **Map Alignment**: Match personal goals with potential career paths and skill requirements.

Reflection: Discuss as a group how the organization's available career paths align with individual goals and what steps can be taken to better align the two.

Worksheet OP3: Internal Mobility Fair

Exercise 2: Internal Mobility Fair

Objective:

To familiarize employees with different departments or roles they could potentially move into.

Materials Needed:

- Presentation booths or stations
- Departmental literature or presentations

Steps:

1. **Preparation**: Each department prepares a brief presentation or information booth.
2. **Event Day**: Employees rotate through the different booths to learn about opportunities in each department.
3. **Interest List**: Employees sign up for roles or projects they're interested in learning more about.

Reflection:

Talk about the experience. Did anything surprise you? Are there new areas of the company you're interested in?

Worksheet OP4: Mentorship Program

Objective:

To provide individualized guidance for career growth.

Materials Needed:

- Mentor and mentee sign-up sheets
- Meeting spaces

Steps:

1. **Sign-Up**: Interested employees sign up as mentors or mentees.
2. **Pairing**: Match mentors with mentees based on career goals and expertise.
3. **Initial Meeting**: Set up an initial meeting to discuss goals and expectations.
4. **Ongoing Meetings**: Schedule regular catch-ups to track progress and adjust goals.

Reflection:

Both mentors and mentees should reflect on what they have gained from the relationship and how it has influenced their professional journey. By consistently incorporating these exercises into your operational routine, you can build an organization where employees feel they have the room and support to grow, ultimately driving engagement and job satisfaction to new heights.

Opportunity

Worksheet OP5: Eisenhower Matrix

Objective:

To help individuals and teams effectively prioritize their daily tasks by categorizing them based on urgency and importance, using the Eisenhower Matrix.

Materials Needed:

- Large whiteboard or poster board - Eisenhower Matrix template (divided into four quadrants: Urgent & Important, Not Urgent & Important, Urgent & Not Important, Not Urgent & Not Important)
- Markers & Sticky notes

Steps:

1. **Introduction to the Eisenhower Matrix:** Briefly explain the concept of the Eisenhower Matrix, detailing the criteria for each quadrant:

    - **Urgent & Important (Do First):** Tasks that require immediate attention and have significant consequences.
    - **Not Urgent & Important (Schedule):** Tasks that are important but do not require immediate action. Planning and setting deadlines for these tasks is crucial.
    - **Urgent & Not Important (Delegate):** Tasks that need to be completed soon but are less important. These can often be delegated to others.
    - **Not Urgent & Not Important (Eliminate):** Tasks that are neither urgent nor important. These should be minimized or eliminated.

2. **List All Tasks:** Each team member writes their current tasks on sticky notes. Encourage them to consider both professional and personal tasks if relevant.

3. **Place Tasks in the Matrix:** Team members place their sticky notes in the appropriate quadrants on the large Eisenhower Matrix on the whiteboard or poster board.

4. **Analyze and Discuss:**
   - Review the tasks in each quadrant.
   - Discuss any surprising placements.
   - Determine if any tasks have been misclassified and need to be moved to a different quadrant.

5. **Action Planning:**
   - **Do First:** Identify which tasks need immediate action and set deadlines.
   - **Schedule:** Decide on a timeline for important, less urgent tasks.
   - **Delegate:** Assign urgent, less important tasks to appropriate team members or plan for delegation.
   - **Eliminate:** Agree on which tasks can be removed from the workload.

6. **Reflection and Commitment:** Each team member reflects on their matrix and commits to specific actions based on their prioritization. Encourage them to take a photo of their personal matrix or replicate it for their workspace.

Reflection:

End the session by reflecting on this prioritization process:

- How does categorizing tasks in this manner affect our view of daily activities?
- Which quadrant was most populated, and what does this tell us about our current work habits?
- How can we regularly incorporate the use of the Eisenhower Matrix into our workflow to enhance productivity and stress management?

Worksheet OP6: Understanding our Purpose

Objective:

To help employees understand and articulate the purpose behind their roles and tasks within the organization.

Materials Needed:

- Pens and notepads
- "Purpose Statement" templates

Steps:

1. **Individual Reflection:** Ask each team member to write down what they believe is the purpose of their role and the tasks they perform.

2. **Share and Discuss:** Create a roundtable setting where each team member shares their thoughts. Discuss similarities and differences in perception of purpose.

3. **Draft Purpose Statements:** Using the "Purpose Statement" templates, guide each team member to draft a refined statement that captures the essence of their role's contribution to the organization's goals.

4. **Group Feedback:** Share the drafted purpose statements with the group for feedback. Use this as an opportunity to clarify and adjust the statements to better reflect organizational objectives and personal values.

5. **Finalize and Display:** Encourage team members to finalize their purpose statements and place them in their workspace as a daily reminder of the value of their work.

Reflection:

Wrap up with a discussion on:

- How does understanding the purpose of our work change our perspective on daily tasks?
- What insights have we gained about the alignment between our roles and the organization's goals?
- How can we maintain a strong sense of purpose moving forward?

Case Study

Unleashing Hidden Potential at "Titan Industrial"

- **The Company:** Titan Industrial Services – they fix, replace, maintain, and even design the massive, dirty machines that are the backbone of power plants, mining operations, and heavy manufacturing. Think less sterile tech, more grease under the fingernails and hard-hat mandatory!

- **The Challenge:** While Titan was thriving, there was a lingering sense of untapped potential. Employees did their jobs well, but engagement surveys spoke of feeling stuck in a rut. Meanwhile, turnover in engineering and skilled trades was rising as some talent was getting poached by flashier, less grimy jobs in tech. Leadership at Titan knew loyalty mattered, but realized "we offer stability" doesn't spark passionate commitment anymore.

- **The Spark:** An honest look in the mirror. Titan discovered it was an ambition killer! Old-school management clung to the mantra "you gotta put in your time". Opportunities existed, but were often filled through external hires, making internal employees feel unvalued and unseen. It wasn't a lack of potential, but a broken path for anyone craving more within the organization.

The Opportunities Offensive

- **The 'Find the Guru' Skill Hunt:** They flipped those job listings inside out. Instead of focusing only on external certifications, leaders brainstormed with veteran staff what made someone truly great at a task. This uncovered unsung masters who possessed immense knowledge, but maybe lacked formal qualifications. This led to creating in-house "certification" programs – tests alongside hands-on scenarios. Suddenly, there was respect and a path forward for these unsung geniuses.

- **"Job Swap Jamboree":** Mandatory 'diversity trainings' got scrapped for something grittier. Annual events allowed engineers to trade places with technicians on the ground, marketing to get filthy learning to repair, even executives shadowed client reps to better grasp real-world pain points. Understanding how every piece fit together fueled empathy and sparked those 'why didn't we think of this?' breakthroughs.

- **The Big Ask - Not the Big Wait:** They blew up passive suggestion boxes. Titan started hosting 'Shark Tank for the Shop Floor' events – anyone could submit an improvement idea, a process bottleneck they wanted to obliterate, a half-baked notion for a new service... messy, often impractical, but EXCITING. Leadership gave real-time feedback, offered support to refine ideas, and YES, some winning concepts got real budgets immediately. Employees' drive shifted – it wasn't about waiting to be noticed, it was proving your idea had merit.

The Impact

- **Retention Boost:** People stopped jumping ship because their internal ambitions kept hitting dead-ends. Titan found that often, what employees wanted wasn't more money, but the chance to tackle exciting challenges within a company they understood and were loyal to.

- **The Untapped Wellspring:** New leaders emerged as their skills became impossible to ignore. Those 'job swap' stints unearthed a marketing wiz who was once a bored technician, while an office admin turned out to have a brilliant grasp of client communication they would never have discovered from her desk.

- **They Got Scrappier (In a Good Way!)**: When every employee started brainstorming improvements, it changed the whole DNA of the place. Titan realized they'd been wasting money and time on inefficient processes no one dared question. Those ideas from the 'shop floor' revolutionized workflows, creating better outcomes all around.

Key Takeaway: Sometimes 'growth opportunity' require less polish and more raw enthusiasm. The grittiest workplaces can still foster a culture where stepping up is always welcomed and the best talent stays – not because they have to, but because they genuinely believe their next big challenge won't require changing companies.

Opportunity

VULNERABILITY

Why Is Practicing Vulnerability Critical to Employee Engagement?

Research by Amy Edmondson, a Harvard Business School professor, proves that teams with a sense of 'psychological safety' outperform those where everyone hides behind a facade of perfection. One such facade is that leaders are tough and thrive on stress.

The tough facade is no longer safe. In *Thrive*, Adrianna Huffington quotes a Harvard Business School study that reported an outrageously high percentage of leaders who said they felt burned out – 96%! If leaders are feeling high stress, imagine what their management team is feeling and then the manager's teams!

Part of practicing vulnerability is to make it safe for everyone to talk about work-life balance that is out of whack, feelings of burn-out, and the need to take a leave of absence to care for a loved one who is facing a life-threatening illness. Hiding life's stresses behind that "I'm tough, bring it on" exterior, is unhealthy, life threatening, and disengaging.

Practicing vulnerability builds trust in the trenches! When leaders acknowledge their stress, it gives others the license to acknowledge it as well. Acknowledgment is the first step toward re-engaging and finding ways to work together to make workplaces safe again.

- After examining hundreds of teams, a study by Google's Project Aristotle revealed psychological safety was the #1 difference distinguishing successful teams and highlighted the impact of vulnerability on team success.
- Psychologically safe workplaces often have lower turnover rates leading to significant cost savings and higher profits by saving the costs of losing employee knowledge and replacing that experienced employee (2024 replacement estimates are up to 2x annual salary).
- In a psychologically safe environment, employees are more likely to be vulnerable and report mistakes without fearing negative consequences or loss of status. The organization can address errors, learn

promptly, and prevent future errors. This not only increases profits and reduces long-term costs, but also can save lives.

Alright, let's remember this more polished corporate-speak as we inject some realness into how you forge a team that trusts each other enough to be vulnerable when the going gets tough.

Vulnerability is about building a team with the courage to get real when the stakes are high.

It's about leaders who own their mistakes, teams who tackle fears head-on, and an environment where asking for help and revealing a mistake is a sign of strength.

Think of vulnerability as the armour for your team's morale, your secret weapon to help everyone keep running strong when change introduces another high hurdle.

KEY OUTCOME

When leaders and employees practice vulnerability, it impacts your bottom line. Feeling safe enough to share concerns, even anxieties, pays off when change throws the next curveball (and you know it will!). Teams practicing vulnerability are secure enough to admit mistakes, ask for backup, and share those risky ideas that might just be a game-changer.

How to Model Vulnerability

Studies show that when leaders admit their own flaws, employees feel more empowered to innovate, knowing that a stumble isn't a career death sentence. Turns out being authentic and trustworthy gains followers. By modelling vulnerability in your organization, you can increase employee engagement and job satisfaction creating more positive and productive work environments. Vulnerability translates into higher retention and productivity, two outcomes with huge positive impacts to your organization's profitability.

- **Show Some Scars:** Leaders, it's time to abandon the "perfect boss" act. Talk about when you made a mistake, about times you felt afraid you were not up to the job at hand, and how you asked for help and received it. You are not showing weakness here but strength. You are sharing how struggling and knowing when you need help are part of success, not something to be hidden.

    Here's a few scenarios to help you show some scars to model vulnerability:

    ### The "Missed Mark" Moment Scenario

    - **Vulnerability WIN:** "Hey team, I totally underestimated the workload on this project. I need another set of hands ASAP to meet the deadline – can someone pitch in, and here's how I'll avoid this overload in the future."

    - **Vulnerability FAIL:** "This project's a nightmare, clients are idiots, and I'm one burnt-out email away from quitting."

Vulnerability

Why it Matters: The first shows ownership, a focus on solutions, and invites collaboration. The second is demoralizing: It focuses on venting and adds to the problem, rather than focusing on fixing it.

Leader's Moment of Realness Scenario

- **Vulnerability WIN:** "This strategy shift is ambitious, and frankly, I don't have all the answers in some areas. Here's what I DO know, here's where your expertise is invaluable, and here's how I'll support getting the answers we don't have yet..."

- **Vulnerability FAIL:** "I'm freaking out about this change, honestly have no clue if we'll pull it off, and am tempted just to play it safe. But that's not why you're here, so let's figure this out together."

Why it Matters: Leaders who show they're not infallible build trust. Honesty, coupled with trust in the team's abilities and a plan of action, invites collaboration.

Panicking creates doubt in your role as a leader and your trust in the team's ability. It invites helplessness.

When we asked for early feedback on this Vulnerability Section, everyone loved the scenarios. So, we created a Bonus Section for Modelling and Coaching Vulnerability at the end of this section. Try using any of the scenarios with Worksheet R4: Create similar realistic examples that fit your context and use them as role plays. Ask team members to add their own examples to make it real for everyone.

How to Coach Vulnerability

Coaching vulnerability creates the rock-solid foundation where no one fears judgment when the plan goes sideways. Your team knows deep down that they're equipped to tackle those curveballs that change throws their way because they can ask for help, rethink strategies, and admit "I don't know...but maybe THIS wild idea could work?"

This doesn't happen overnight. Building this kind of trust is a constant effort. And the reward? A team that's as resilient as they are ambitious, one that weathers those "change storms" that sweep others away.

Here are some ways executives and managers coach their teams to practice vulnerability:

Leaders and Managers Celebrate Failure

- **Fail Spectacularly, Share Bravely:** When managers normalize missteps as expected events in the workplace, team members no longer need to hide them. They can share their failures to help others learn right along with them. No need for everyone to make the same misstep! So don't just talk about what went right – mine those glorious failures. Dedicate time in meetings for team members to share stumbles and the valuable (often hilarious) lessons learned.

  The "Aha" vs. the "Ouch" Scenario

    - **Vulnerability WIN:** "So, that experiment flopped, but here's the surprising thing that DID happen, which could lead to [new angle]. Thoughts on if this is worth pursuing more?"

- **Vulnerability FAIL:** "I screwed up that project. I knew I shouldn't have tried that, I always mess up, guess I'm just not cut out for this kind of risk-taking."

Why it Matters: Emphasize "productive failure." Focus on the learning, even the humor of the misstep, to allay fears about trying bold things. Dwelling on self-blame shuts that innovation down.

Use Worksheet V2 to practice failure stories. Kick it off with your personal story of an experiment that flopped and what you learned from it. Your team will feel safe to try innovative ideas and share failures to get more ideas.

Bonus Tip! Everyone can learn from each other's failures! No need to duplicate a failure on this team!

When Plans Need to Pivot Scenario

- **Vulnerability WIN**: "Our original strategy hit a roadblock—here's the data showing why. Based on this, I propose we shift direction to [new approach]. I'm open to alternatives, but inaction isn't an option."
- **Vulnerability FAIL**: "Well, that plan was a bust! Guess I'll brainstorm something else alone, you all just wait for new instructions."

Vulnerability

Why it Matters: Sharing the 'why' behind the shift demystifies decision-making. It admits a misstep, but then positions you as a fellow problem-solver who invite input while retaining ownership of the path forward.

NOTE: This is the strategy pivot mentioned in Worksheet V4. Is this a good example to use with your teams?

- **Psychological Safety = Survival Mode:** Coach your teams to ask tough questions and express concerns, even if unpopular. This is how to build trust and avoid disaster as a team. Take time to address eye rolls and sarcastic remarks, offline if needed. If you don't, the best ideas may stay under wraps.

Managers Cultivate Trust, the Real Kind

- **Team Spirit Is Not Just About After-work BBQs:** If your teams dread after-hour team-building efforts that take time away from their families or hobbies, please forego them. Real trust builds when teams are tackling tough challenges side-by-side. Mix up project teams, enable unlikely allies to collaborate, and celebrate shared wins with genuine enthusiasm.

- **Feedback That Fuels, Not Burns:** Teach everyone, especially leaders, how to give constructive feedback that helps, not humiliates. Focus on specific behaviors, impact, and offer suggestions for alternatives. Dump those vague "you need to improve" slams.

Vulnerability

Learning from the "Rookie" Scenario

- **Vulnerability WIN**: [To a junior team member] "Looks like you've mastered [new software] way faster than I have. Mind showing me your approach? Old dogs can learn new tricks, after all."

- **Vulnerability FAIL**: [Resentfully] "Guess I'm obsolete now, since a newbie's better at this than I am. Might as well start polishing my resume."

Why it Matters: Acknowledging another's expertise is powerful, even when it stings a bit. Humility and a focus on self-improvement preserve respect and model a growth mindset for everyone.

Try Worksheet V3. Kick it off with your own constructive feedback to a junior team member in the Learning from the "Rookie: Scenario. Ask the team to give positive feedback to team members who have mastered a new skill and ask them to share what they have learned.

We have seen this scenario turn into a "Lunch 'n' Learn" session for the whole team!

- **Empathy is Your Superpower:** People gotta feel understood, not just instructed. Dedicate time to learning about teammates' backgrounds, the struggles they faced, and what fuels their passions. This is where those "extra effort" moments come from when deadlines get brutal.

Here is a scenario that can help you practice empathy with a team member who seems a bit off today:

Vulnerability

When Empathy is Needed Scenario

- **Vulnerability WIN:** "Hey [teammate], I noticed you seem a bit off lately. This is a tough stretch – anything I can do to support you? Or if you're not ready to talk, know I'm here when you are."

- **Vulnerability FAIL:** "Is everything okay? You seem distracted recently, and it's impacting the work. What's going on with you?"

Why it Matters: Showing concern is powerful, but respect boundaries. Offering an open door beats demanding explanations. This builds the safety net where folks are more likely to ask for help when truly needed.

Extra Coaching Tip: Share some "statement starters" to help you and your team practice healthy vulnerability:

- "I'm struggling with...",
- "I could use a second opinion on...",
- "Here's what I've learned from this setback..."

Coaching vulnerability makes it less intimidating for folks who aren't used to operating this way. Try using Worksheet V1 and get it started with these starters!

How to Reward Vulnerability Wins

Vulnerability has its own intrinsic rewards over time. In the meantime, you can make their efforts obvious to others, offer encouragement, and show appreciation for small and large strides along the way. So, while you are maturing your vulnerability practice and waiting for the intrinsic rewards to kick in, take time to recognize individual and team efforts to let their guard down.

Recognize Vulnerability Wins:

- **"Wins" are currency:** Did an individual or the whole team known for working solo ask for help? Did it have a positive impact on a challenging deliverable? Invite the team to share their success story at the next all team meeting. Try Workshop #3 to prepare for the all hands.

- **Create a Vulnerability Memory Board**: In the early days, teams may not recognize the progress they are making. Or they may show vulnerable moments and then regress to presenting their old cold-hearted steely armours. Create a Vulnerability Memory Board to remind the teams of their progress. For a maturing team who has done Vulnerability Circles (Worksheet V1) at the beginning of their practice, hold another one and ask them how it feels different than that first time.

- **Worksheet V1 Gone Sticky**: Use the Vulnerability Circle Worksheet V1 and the "Feeling Stuck" scenario below to practice asking for help sooner rather than later when we are "stuck".

First share the "Feeling Stuck" Scenario below. Then share your own challenge and ask for specific help - without calling yourself a dummy. Ask if anyone else on the team is feeling stuck and give them space to practice asking for help while making it specific - and without self-deprecation.

Appreciation is a great reward!! Thank the helpers, the askers, and the team for unblocking important work.

"Feeling Stuck" Scenario:

- **Vulnerability WIN:** "I'm hitting a wall on this [specific task]. Has anyone tackled something similar before and could offer a fresh perspective? Or maybe there's a resource I'm overlooking..."
- **Vulnerability FAIL:** "I'm so dumb, I can't figure this out, and I'm going to get fired."

Why it's important: Asking for help is powerful especially when it is specific. Self-deprecation shuts down support. Focusing on the actual problem lets someone offer the needed assistance. Don't forget to thank your helper!

Take time to reward teams and individuals who changed their outlooks from maintaining a tough exterior to inviting collaboration, laughing at their own mistakes, and taking risks.

How to Celebrate Vulnerability

There are always moments in a new practice when we revert to the old ways of working. Celebrating our awareness of our backslides removes blame and encourages learning. This extra step can harden the connection between vulnerability and engagement.

- **Celebrate the Backslides:** If we can name a backslide, we can learn from it. And we can learn from each other's backslides. Try Worksheet V2 and rename it Backslide Stories.

- Add Backslide Moments to the Vulnerability Memory Board created in the last section.

- **Celebrate the Trendline**: What are some ways you can quantify how vulnerability is making a positive difference? Have we reduced the time we stew over a challenge by asking for help? Have we reduced rework by stepping out of our siloes and collaborating with another team? When we sent a team member home who is tending to a sick loved one, did we feel energized and happy about adding their work to the team's workload? These are proper milestones in our vulnerability maturity. Celebrate them visibly on the Vulnerability Memory Board.

How to Sustain Vulnerability

Turns out, the best teams fight constructively. Research by Jennifer Mueller of the University of San Diego shows that a little respectful conflict fuels creative solutions precisely because everyone's not afraid to butt heads in service of a better outcome. When you're not wasting energy hiding mistakes, those disagreements become catalysts for success, not nails in the coffin of team morale. Let's try some constructive conflict scenarios here:

The Constructive Clash Scenario

- **Vulnerability WIN**: "I respect your approach, but here's why I think [alternative] might be a stronger play, based on [data or past experience]."

- **Vulnerability FAIL**: "This whole idea is terrible, you always do it this way and it always fails, what's wrong with you?"

Why it Matters: Respectful disagreement fuels growth, but there's a difference between challenging ideas and attacking the person behind them.

Have the constructive clash in private. Then role play the clash together using Worksheet V3 to celebrate constructive feedback. Encourage team members to practice what they saw.

Don't underestimate the ripple effect of sustained vulnerability! Studies prove that **customers** can sense the difference between a team operating from fear and one energized by that sense of safety and shared purpose.

How to Rescue Failing Vulnerability Practices

Vulnerability + Professionalism Gotta Coexist: Fostering vulnerability doesn't mean turning the workplace into a non-stop group therapy session. Here's how to strike that balance:

- **Boundaries Matter, Even When You're Real:**

    Vulnerability in the service of the team isn't an excuse for oversharing. Guidelines are king! Think specific work-related challenges ("This new process is driving me nuts"), admitting knowledge gaps ("I need help on this..."), or owning up to missteps that impacted others. Keep personal life drama, venting about annoying coworkers, or armchair psychologist moments for outside work hours.

- **Sharing with Purpose, Not Just to Complain:**

    Vulnerability is a tool, not a whine-fest. Focus on solutions or what you're LEARNING from a tough experience. "This project's a mess, and here's where I think I messed up" opens a productive door. "This project sucks" slams it shut.

- **Respect is the Bedrock:**

    Empathy doesn't mean tolerating unprofessional behavior. It's okay to have hard conversations even amidst a culture of honesty. Leaders, especially, need to model this – they still hold people accountable. The difference? It's not humiliating; it's clear, specific, and focused on finding a better way forward together.

- **HR managers, Step Up Your Game:** Lip service to vulnerability doesn't hack it. Your HR team needs to be trained to support employees choosing vulnerability. They should be champions of fairness, not enforcers of rigid rules.

NEXT UP! By popular demand, we are including BONUS SCENARIOS to help you recognize yourself and others in the Vulnerability Scenario WINS and FAILS. Considering personalities and potential hurdles, can you brainstorm how to kickstart WINS in your company and context? WINS pack a lot more power when they are tailored to your people and context.

Modelling and Coaching Vulnerability in Real Life
Bonus Scenarios

How does Vulnerability Apply to YOU? Whether you are a middle manager, senior manager or C-Suite Executive, practicing vulnerability will gain the prize of trust from other managers and their teams. You can start the riptide to increase engagement, productivity and happiness on the job at all levels!

Middle Management Vulnerability "WINS":

The "What's My Job Now?" Moment Scenario

- **Vulnerability WIN**: [Addressing their team] "Alright folks, this shift to [new process] is a big change. I'm still figuring out how my role best supports you all – here's what I'm thinking so far, but open to your input on what would be most helpful."

- **Vulnerability FAIL:** "I have no idea how I'm useful anymore. This new system sucks, and I'm lost. Anyone else feel the same?"

Why it Matters: Admitting uncertainty humanizes you. Following immediately with proactive steps to find your place in the new system sets an important example. It invites collaboration instead of inviting everyone to a pity party.

When you model how to respond to big changes to your role, you may be giving them one of the best lessons in their professional careers. When you share your thoughts and ask for their input, you are building trust that you have a plan on how to bounce back and want to help them be resilient to the change as well. Your vulnerability will definitely impact their own response to the current change and can teach them how to respond to changes in the future.

The Overburdened Buffer Scenario

- **Vulnerability WIN:** [To their superior] "I'm getting pulled in many directions with these changes. I need help prioritizing which requests from my team are essential and which can wait...otherwise, I'm becoming the bottleneck, not the facilitator."

- **Vulnerability FAIL:** [Exhausted & exasperated] "I'm just the messenger getting yelled at from both sides! No one gets how hard this is. Should I just give everyone your direct contact so you can all fight it out?"

Why it Matters: Asking for strategic support is vulnerable and is highly effective when you frame it as essential support needed to help your teams be successful. Venting may be tempting, but ultimately makes managers look ineffective.

Bonus "Power Moves" for Middle Management:

- Seek out a "Reverse Mentor": Find a junior team member who thrives in the new system, and actively learn from them. This flips the old hierarchy in a constructive way.

- Host "Fail Fest" Share Sessions: Dedicate time for everyone (including you) to fess up to a change-related flub. Humor + learning from what went wrong eases tension across the board.

  Try Worksheet V2 and label it "Fail Fest" or "Fun with Flubs".

- Publicly THANK Upwards: Acknowledging times when senior leadership directly supported the team's adaptation to this new model bolsters trust on both sides.

  Use Worksheet V3 and invite your senior leader to attend to receive thanks for their support.

Upper Leadership Vulnerability "Wins":

Addressing The "Why Are We Doing This?" Frustration Scenario

- **Vulnerability WIN:** "This transformation is demanding. I know change fatigue is real, I feel it too. Here's what hasn't been communicated clearly enough—why this is worth the struggle, the bigger picture it serves [link to company's mission]..."

- **Vulnerability FAIL**: "To be honest, this change was forced on us [by market shifts, etc.]. It's tough, but we gotta figure it out. So suck it up and get on board."

Vulnerability

Why it Matters: Acknowledging the difficulty builds empathy. But crucially, this is followed by WHY it matters, connecting the pain to purpose. Brutal honesty without vision is demoralizing.

Look at Worksheet V4: Does this Vulnerability FAIL fit your organization? If so, adapt it as a role play using the Vulnerability WIN above.

The "I Don't Know, But Let's Find Out" Moment Scenario

- **Vulnerability WIN:** "That's a great question on [complex issue] and I don't have a ready answer. What I DO have are resources committed to researching this, including your expertise. Let's figure this out together."

- **Vulnerability FAIL:** [Blustering/faking expertise] "Don't worry about it, I've got this handled. Just focus on your specific tasks."

Why it Matters: No one expects leaders to know everything, but they DO expect them to facilitate solutions. This shows they trust their team's collective intelligence.

See Worksheet V4: Is this a good role play scenario for your team?

Upper Leadership "Bonus Moves":

- Celebrate "Productive Failure" Company-Wide: Highlight a leader who took a calculated risk that didn't pan out,

Vulnerability

but what they LEARNED from it was invaluable. This signals that it's okay to not be perfect.

- The "Ask Me Anything" Open Forum: Set time where no question is off-limits. This requires thick skin, but demonstrates willingness to address the unspoken anxieties head-on.

- Showcase a Leader's, or Perhaps Your Own Learning Curve: Mention a new skill a leader is struggling with or a mentor they sought out. Show that even at the top, growth is a constant process.

If you recognize yourself in the Vulnerability FAILS: Don't Despair! Give yourselves an A for Awareness and use your FAIL to help others learn with you. Then commit to practice a Vulnerability WIN today.

Will you FAIL again? Sure! Pick yourself up, Dust yourself off, and celebrate another learning opportunity. You are on the road to building trust with your teams. They will reward your effort and join in.

 Grab Your Compass!

 Hit The Pause Button!

Review the worksheets below and add them to your Vulnerability Practice. Let us know what works and what doesn't work for you or your context. We are always anxious to hear from you.

Worksheets

Vulnerability

Vulnerability

Worksheet V1: Vulnerability Circle

Objective:

To create a safe space where team members can share personal experiences and challenges openly.

Materials Needed:

- A quiet, comfortable room
- Timer

Steps:

1. **Ground Rules**: Establish rules to ensure confidentiality and respectful listening.
2. **Opening**: One person starts by sharing a personal challenge or experience they feel comfortable discussing.
3. **Time Limit**: The speaker has 3 minutes to speak. No one is allowed to interrupt.
4. **Listening**: Everyone else listens attentively without forming judgments or responses.
5. **Rotate**: The next person in the circle shares, and the process continues until everyone has had a chance to speak.

Reflection:

How did it feel to share and to listen? Do you feel closer or more trusting of your team members?

Vulnerability

Worksheet V2: Failure Stories

Objective:

To normalize failure as a part of the learning process.

Materials Needed:

- Whiteboard or flip chart
- Markers

Steps:

1. **Prompt**: Ask team members to think of a time they failed at something in their professional life.
2. **Sharing**: Volunteers share their failure stories, focusing on what they learned from the experience.
3. **List Learnings**: Write down the key takeaways from each story.

Reflection:

Discuss how failure has contributed to individual and team growth. How can the team better support each other in times of failure?

Vulnerability

Worksheet V3: Feedback Roulette

Objective:

To practice giving and receiving constructive feedback.

Materials Needed:

- Paper
- Pens
- A bowl or container

Steps:

1. Write Feedback: Each person writes anonymous constructive feedback for every other team member on separate pieces of paper.
2. Collect: Place all feedback notes in a bowl.
3. Distribute: Everyone draws a piece of feedback from the bowl.
4. Read: Team members read the feedback they received.
5. Discussion: Open floor for general reflections and discussions.

Reflection:

How did it feel to give and receive feedback in this manner? Was the feedback surprising or expected? How can you use this feedback to grow?

Vulnerability

Worksheet V4: Leadership Archetypes

Objective:

To foster a company culture where vulnerability is seen as a tool for growth, resilience, and innovation. This objective includes:

- Empowering leaders to model vulnerability in a way that balances honesty with maintaining authority and trust.
- Providing employees with guidelines on sharing constructively in a professional context.
- Establishing a safe and supportive environment where expressing concerns, admitting mistakes, and asking for help are seen as strengths, not weaknesses.

Materials Needed:

- Discussion Prompts: These spark team conversations about change, failure, and moments they wish communication had been more open. Prompts should vary in intensity to ease into deeper concepts over time.

Steps:

1. Leader Archetypes

Think of 3-4 broad personality types you typically see amongst your upper leadership:

- The "Stoic Strategist": Data-driven, logical, might be perceived as lacking emotion.
- The "Visionary Charmer": Big on inspiration, can be light on detail follow-through.
- The "Old Guard Veteran": Values experience, might struggle with tech/cultural shifts.

Vulnerability

- Any other dominant types within your company?

2. Vulnerability Comfort Zones

For each archetype, ask yourself:

- Where are they naturally good at showing honesty? (Perhaps admitting gaps in technical knowledge, but not emotional struggles?)
- What would feel most AGAINST their personality? (A hug-it-out type of sharing session might make the Stoic Strategist cringe)

3. Scenario Matching

Let's take one of those scenarios from our earlier examples – like the need for a strategy pivot – and tailor it to different personalities:

- Stoic Strategist: Emphasizes the data driving the change, invites discussion of options, but within set parameters. Vulnerability lies in admitting the original path was flawed, not in showing personal disappointment.
- Visionary Charmer: Focuses on the exciting new possibilities change unlocks. Their vulnerability is admitting they need the team's help making the vision tangible, with less emphasis on the original plan's shortcomings.
- Old Guard Veteran: Leans on their experience to explain the changing landscape, emphasizing that their goal is to ensure the company (and its people) not just survive, but thrive. Their vulnerability is admitting they don't have all the answers for HOW that happens in this new world.

Additional Notes:

- Rollout is Key: This can't be a one-time workshop. Integrate vulnerability concepts into ongoing meetings, leadership development, and as situations arise naturally within teams.

Vulnerability

- Tailored is Better: Generic vulnerability training is less effective. Use your company's lingo, past wins/fails as examples, and address the specific anxieties your people feel during change.
- Feedback Loop: Track how perceptions of "psychological safety" change over time through surveys or focused discussions. Adjust your approach as needed.

Case Study

Forging Trust in the Vault

How Titan National Bank Built a Culture Where Vulnerability Wasn't a Liability.

The Challenge: Titan National Bank was steady as an old safe – and just as change-resistant. Processes were rigid, hierarchy ruled, and while employees rarely screwed up publicly, neither did they take the calculated risks that could lead to truly innovative services. Then, those pesky fintech upstarts started chipping away at their market share. Titan's leadership realized that a bunker mentality wouldn't cut it anymore – they needed a team that felt secure enough to suggest crazy ideas, own up to mistakes quickly, and navigate inevitable client frustrations with empathy instead of defensiveness.

The Vulnerability Offensive:

- **Leader's Under the Microscope**: No more pretending the CEO had all the answers. She began company-wide meetings by admitting a recent strategic fumble, followed by what she was doing differently because of it. This set off a chain reaction, with managers hesitantly (then boldly) following suit.

Vulnerability

- **The Fail Fest**: Not a pity party! These were short, snappy, even humorous team spotlights on how a misstep led to unexpected improvement. It began with showcasing "safe" process tweaks, but quickly escalated to admitting client relationship blunders, showing that honesty was rewarded, not career-ending.

- **"Help Wanted" Brainstorm Boards**: Instead of agonizing in silos, teams posted challenges on a dedicated space (physical and digital). Asking for help became normalized, and those who offered a fresh perspective were publicly praised – even when their solution wasn't the final winner.

- **The "Feelings...with Follow-Through" Approach:** Leaders focused on reframing empathy. It wasn't about coddling upset clients, but channeling their frustration into actionable changes. Employees were taught to say, "I understand that's incredibly frustrating. Here's what I CAN do, and what I'll take to my team to find a better way..."

The Impact:

- **Ideas That Seemed Nuts, but Worked**: A bored teller turned social media whiz revamped their online presence with sassy, informative posts, attracting a younger clientele. A branch manager's "wild idea" for a community outreach program built stronger local business partnerships than expensive conventional advertising.

Vulnerability

- **Screw-Ups Didn't Derail**: A botched regulatory reporting error was caught early because the team member responsible fessed up, allowing for immediate correction. This led to revamping overly complex procedures that were setting everyone up for potential failure.

- **Client Loyalty Got Stickier**: Turns out, when customers felt truly heard – even when the answer was "no" – the relationship remained strong. Complaints on review sites decreased, and referrals from existing clients increased due to proactive problem-solving and honest communication, even in tough situations.

Key Takeaway:

Building vulnerability-as-strength into a conservative industry like banking isn't easy. Titan Bank learned that it's not about "sharing feelings" but tangible actions that prove they trust their people to handle the tough stuff. Respect is paramount, and that meant clear guidelines, support systems, and follow-through on those moments of vulnerability to show that taking those risks is how everyone wins.

Additional Thoughts:

Vulnerability in Action for the Banking Sector

- **Cybersecurity Breaches**: The instinct is to hide mistakes, fearing reputational damage. But, a culture of quickly admitting issues leads to faster containment and mitigation. Train employees to immediately escalate anomalies, however minor, with the promise of focusing on solutions, not blame.

- **Client Data Concerns**: Instead of defensive legalese when questioned, proactively inform clients about how their data is used, including its limitations. Offer opt-outs when feasible. This builds trust even when the answers aren't ideal from the consumer's perspective.

- **Shifting Financial Needs**: Train staff at all levels to admit when they don't know the best product for a client's unique situation. This shouldn't lead to a shrug, but a facilitated connection to someone who DOES have the expertise – even if it's a specialist at another branch.

- **"We've Always Done it This Way" Syndrome**: Create a pitch process where anyone can submit a process improvement idea, no matter their title. Make the focus on clear ROI and feasibility, not just questioning the status quo for its own sake. These wins can fuel momentum for a less stagnant workflow overall.

- **Remote Work Resistance:** Many banking roles still cling to rigid in-office models. Experiment with teams where transparency becomes key. Instead of micromanaging hours, set shared goals and let the team prove that flexibility is possible, while maintaining those iron-clad security standards.

Vulnerability

ENABLEMENT

Why is Enablement Critical to Employee Engagement?

Empowering employees to make decisions and enabling them to do their work with the latest tools and technologies boosts engagement. It gives them a sense of ownership in their organizations' solutions and the sense their work is connected to the greater "Why". It is about clearing the path so your people can charge forward, unblocked by bureaucracy, legacy technologies, and outdated policies. It allows them to optimize workflows for delivery to customers and ensures all employees feel their voice MATTERS in this process.

A study by Kotter International found a **682% average increase in revenue growth** for 12 organizations with performance-enhancing cultures.

KEY OUTCOME

People don't just feel heard, they feel UNSTOPPABLE. They know leadership no longer tolerates roadblocks and is actively clearing the way for their efforts to truly shine. They feel their organization is delegating effectively and setting their employees up for success.

How to Model Enablement

Employees look to their managers to empower them with the tools, technology, information and training they need to do their jobs. They also need the authority to make the decisions that require their specific knowledge to make the right decision for the desired outcome. Managers can optimize engagement using important enablement moves:

- Connect the work to the "Why"
- Remove barriers
- Optimize **ways of working** for efficient performance
- Use knowledge where the work happens to make decisions about that work
- Identify Legacy Practices that block work
- Remove legacy practices that hinder progress
- Prioritize high impact projects

Your Armory for Enabling Your Team's Full Potential:

Connect the Work to the "Why":

Managers, you are your employee's connection to the higher purpose of their organizations.

- **More to come here.**

Weaponizing Resources: Beyond the Bare Minimum

- **Tech Upgrades Are a Must, Not a Nice to Have**: If software is from the dark ages, or systems crash constantly, invest in upgrades instead of wishful thinking! But don't just throw new tools at people!

- **Provide hands-on training**: Dedicate time, training and support for your teams to master the new systems. Proactively avoid frustrated cursing at a new complex tool that no one can figure out how to use.

- **Expertise On Tap for Knowledge Transfers**: Tap into external consultants with the specialized knowledge to train internal staff. Explicitly state in their contract that you are paying them to train the staff to do the work themselves. Throughout their engagement, require frequent demos to show how your staff can use the important functionality for these expensive new tools. A fancy slide deck no one understands when they leave is not the outcome you require.

- **Create a Centralized Knowledge Repository**: Information shouldn't require a time-intensive Scavenger Hunt. If vital stuff is buried in forgotten SharePoint folders or only shared at meetings, some miss in their time zone, precious time is wasted, and morale plummets. Create a centralized hub where policies, process updates, Nonfunctional Requirements, Coding Standards, Definition of Done, and other essential knowledge are easily accessible. Make your teams accountable for updating and adding new artifacts to the repository. Your goal is to stop the vicious cycle of demoralizing searches for inaccessible but necessary information. Take time to capture the treasure of reusable knowledge you have! Duplication is wasteful.

How to Coach Enablement

Dismiss the Micromanagement Monster

- **"Ownership" Isn't Just a Buzzword**: Coach your people to own the work and the goals. You've enabled them to make decisions, use new tools and technologies, and maintain a knowledge repository. Now, you can get out of their way. If micromanaging every step was effective, we'd all have time for a three-hour lunch. Knowledge workers are motivated by outcomes, not by the constant need to seek approval for their next solution.

- **Coach them to Question Ridiculous Rules**: Is there a policy just because it's always been there? Empower people to question the "we've always done it this way" quagmire. A bonfire of outdated regulations can be incredibly freeing – and often reveals significant cost-savings by freeing up the red tape.

- **Decisions, Decisions**: Are there areas where you actually CAN push decision-making down the chain? Can you give teams budget authority for small expenses and let frontline employees resolve those "easy fix" customer issues without escalating to a manager? Be ready to coach the teams on these new decision-making responsibilities, as they may be ready but unprepared for their new role. The ability to make fast decisions that rely on their knowledge builds confidence, reduces frustrating wait times, accelerates product development, and frees leaders to focus on the bigger strategic plays they are paid to make.

The Growth Crusade: Unleashing Ambition

- **"Potential" is Meaningless Without a Plan**: Don't just say you value professional development; coach your employees to create their personal pathways for professional development. Give them a budget for online courses and conferences that spark fresh thinking. Review their development plans in the weekly check-ins you adopted in the Communication Section. Reach out to other managers to coordinate rotational job-share programs where people can dip their toes into different pools of knowledge and expertise at your company.

- **Mentorship Matters**: Coach those hungry for growth to pair with experienced folks who have a knack for teaching or have vast knowledge in their interest areas. Save this reward for motivated, ambitious learners, and be wary of unmotivated naysayers who will waste a mentor's time.

How to Reward Enabled Workers

You can build a culture where positivity is powerful. Recognize and reward the great strides your employees make as you enable them to excel—not just in your private weekly check-ins but also publicly so the whole team is cheering them on!

- **Victory Laps Required**: Reward milestones along the way, not just at the final finish line that seems a million miles away. Frequent rewards for small but essential milestones remind everyone why the tough stuff is worth it. Your goal is to keep their spirits high especially when everyone knows the next change is just around the bend.

- **Highlight the "Unsung Heroes":** Who's the quiet genius behind that new streamlined process? The person who continuously diffuses client's anger? Make those often-overlooked contributions known company-wide.

- **A Little Fun Goes a Long Way**: Mandatory "fun days" are often forced. But spontaneous moments of levity are powerful. Try a ridiculous trophy for the most epic self-reported tech fail or a contest to uncover the silliest outdated policy. Find what fits your team's humor!

    o **Growth Beyond Titles**: Maybe everyone can't be VP overnight. Reward your ambitious employees who step up to lead special projects, gain mastery in a niche skill, or take calculated risks that push beyond their job description. Recognize those efforts just as enthusiastically as a promotion with a new title.

- **Recognize Talent Beyond the Org Chart:**

    Titles mean squat. That quiet genius tucked away in a boring-sounding role might have the insights to revolutionize a process. Find out what gets folks fired up beyond their current tasks.

    o **Make Positivity a Priority**: Yeah, change is hard, but a constant doom-and-gloom vibe is a self-fulfilling prophecy. Celebrate even small wins enthusiastically and keep morale from nosediving when setbacks happen.

- **Work HARD, Live WELL:** Use flexibility whenever possible to support well-being. Show that you know they are not robots and that some aspects of their role are extra demanding during the transformation process.

- **Visible good ideas are rewarding. Vanishing good ideas are demoralizing**: If people suggest improvements, there needs to be a visible system for tracking them, not just a dusty suggestion box. Publicly recognize, review, and IMPLEMENT those brilliant notions that come from unexpected places.

Work-Life Balance Rewards: Sanity Saves the Day

- **Flexibility Where Possible**: This ain't about everyone working from a beach hut. But could some roles have staggered hours, remote options when it makes sense, or the ability to truly switch off during non-work hours without guilt? This shows you value them as whole humans.

- **Burnout is the Enemy**: Watch for those "always on" heroes. Sometimes, mandating time off is necessary. And if workloads are chronically insane during the transformation, be honest about that and its temporary nature. People will tolerate a sprint but not a never-ending marathon to nowhere.

Enablement

- **Leaders, Walk the Walk**: Do execs brag about never taking a vacation or answering emails at midnight? That trickles down and creates a toxic culture. If those at the top model a healthy balance, it gives everyone else "permission" to prioritize well-being too.

How to Celebrate Enablement Gains

- **Celebrate Realistic Gains Iteratively**
    - **Celebrate frequent gains frequently**: A few focused "enablement" actions done well every quarter is the goal. Remember, change fatigue sets in for leaders, too! Don't try to fix and celebrate everything at once. Instead, send frequent messages about frequent WINs. This is more powerful than a vague laundry list of planned gains.
    - **Transparency is your friend**: Be upfront about what you CAN and CANNOT change (at least in the short term). This builds trust even when you don't have all the solutions yet.
    - **Track those wins and make them visible to your teams:** Did a new communication process cut down on pointless meetings? Did that tech upgrade result in faster client turnaround? Make sure these successes are visible, as it justifies further efforts (and gets buy-in from initial skeptics).

- **Celebrate the Spectacular Screw-Up**
    - Hold a "Fail Fest" where teams present their most epic blunders during the change process... AND what they learned from it.
    - Make it humorous, with prizes for "Most Preventable" or "So Bad It's Brilliant" fails.
    - Make it fun! Gamify the Fail Fest with silly prizes, "Roast the Leader" sessions, or whatever fits your company's vibe. The more you celebrate them, the closer you will come to the cultural shift you are after.

- **Key Takeaways:**
    - Humor lessens fear, enabling people to try bold things.
    - Lessons gained enable everyone to improve faster.
    - Messing up is an expected part of the enablement process!

How to Sustain Enablement

Enablement needs constant refreshes to keep it vital and engaging to your employees. You've invested heavily in your roles to model, coach, reward, and celebrate enablement for your teams. Let's explore ways you can sustain your team's enablement goals.

The Pain Point Audit

- **Gather the troops**: Don't just rely on your own observations.
    - Hold focused listening sessions with a mix of employees from various levels and departments.
    - Ask specifically: "What's ONE obstacle if removed, would make your job significantly easier/more fulfilling during this time of change?"
    - Create an Obstacle Removal Roadmap and share it with your teams to see if they have any additional thoughts.
    - Ask them to help you prioritize their obstacles and pain points based on urgency and impact in upcoming activities.
- **Quantify the misery**: Can your teams help you track how much time is wasted due to outdated tech, redundant processes, or miscommunication? Ask them to consider the obstacles they noted in the last exercise. Numbers sometimes get action where vague complaints fail. Pair this with the
- **The "little things" matter**: Big systemic changes are important, but don't underestimate seemingly minor annoyances. Fixing the always-broken coffee machine might seem silly, but it can have a disproportionate effect on morale when everything else feels like a struggle.

Enablement

- **Prioritize Your Empowerment Battles: Your action plan**
    - **High Impact, Quick Wins**: What can you change relatively easily, that will have an immediate positive effect? Getting rid of a pointless weekly report everyone hates fits here. Sometimes, these quick victories create momentum for tackling the bigger beasts.
    - **The Root Cause Killers**: Is there a core problem that's causing multiple headaches downstream? Poor communication between departments might be the culprit behind delays, duplicated work, and low morale. Fixing THAT has a ripple effect.
    - **What's Within Your Control**: Restructuring the whole company might be the dream, but is it realistic right now? Focus on areas where leadership can truly make a difference, avoiding the temptation to deflect blame onto forces beyond your influence.
    - **Don't Go it Alone**: Who are your potential allies in this fight? Are there well-respected folks in IT who'd love to upgrade systems, or an HR rep who's also passionate about mentorship programs? Build coalitions for greater firepower.

Thinking about specific areas in the organization

Issue #1: Lack of Communication

- Quick Fix: Death to jargon-filled memos! If employees need a decoder ring to understand updates, it's not good communication. Challenge leaders to use plain language and focus on the "WHY" behind decisions.

- Longer-term: Two-way streets are essential. Create an "Ask Me Anything" channel with dedicated times for responses. Could be a Slack thread, open forum, or even anonymous if fear is a factor. Ignoring the chatter is a recipe for disaster.

Issue #2: Siloed Organization

- Quick Fix: "Speed Dating" for Teams. Short, focused meetings where different departments pitch a current challenge they face and others brainstorm out-the-box solutions. Forces a peek outside their usual bubble.

- Longer-term: Mixed-up project teams. Instead of the usual suspects always working together, form groups with diverse skill sets and departments represented. Freshens perspective AND breaks down those "us vs. them" mentalities.

Issue #3: Confused Middle Management

- Quick Fix: Give 'em a safe space. A safe forum specifically for middle managers to vent frustrations upwards, without consequences. This ISN'T about whining, but surfacing trends leadership may be missing at the ground level.

- Longer-term: They need the master plan. Are they trained on HOW to implement change, or just given the change itself to enforce? Invest in workshops or resources focused on change management skills.

Issue # 4: Change Fatigue

- Quick Fix: The "Pause for Competence." Once a big change is in place, dedicate time to truly MASTERING the new process/skill BEFORE rolling out the next thing. This builds confidence, which fuels the stamina for further change.

- Longer-term: Kill Zombie Projects. Are there low-impact initiatives dragging on just because they "started"? Be ruthless about prioritizing. Clearing the decks frees up mental energy!

Issue #5: Too Busy

- Quick Fix: Meeting Massacre! Have everyone track their hours spent in meetings for a week. Then, challenge the necessity of each one. Could it be an email? Cut in half? Sometimes sheer volume is the soul-sucker. Take a look at Worksheet R7 in the next section.

- Longer-term: "Protect the Focus Time." Can certain afternoons be "meeting free" zones? Allowing for stretches of uninterrupted work gets more done than an over-scheduled calendar with no time to actually execute.

A Few Caveats:

- Your mileage may vary! What's a 'quick fix' depends on your company's size and complexity
- Culture is key: If cynicism runs deep, even well-intentioned actions will be met with suspicion. This is where small, but consistent, wins build trust over time.

How to Rescue Failing Enablement Practices

Hold Hackathons for the Hated Procedures

- The Concept: Declare war on soul-crushing processes! Instead of the usual idea hackathon, teams gather to obliterate a particularly loathed procedure. They analyze its pain points, dissect why it exists in the first place, then go into full-on competitive mode to design a better solution.
- Why it Works: Combines the energy of competition with actually solving a common frustration. Make those prizes for the winning team worth fighting for (a ridiculous trophy, extra time off, or even just bragging rights can be powerful).
- Key to Success: Leadership MUST be in the trenches. They're part of the hacking teams, and their buy-in to implement the winning solution is non-negotiable. This proves it's more than a fun exercise.

"Red Tape Roast"

- The Concept: Think open mic night, but for venting bureaucracy-induced misery. Set the stage with comically oversized scissors, a fake bonfire, whatever gets people into the spirit of tearing down pointless rules. Each rant is timeboxed to stay focused, followed by a lightning round for potential fixes.

- Why it Works: Humor breaks tension, but the core purpose is serious. Leaders scribbling furiously during the rants shows they're not just tolerating criticism, but truly listening for areas where immediate action is possible.

- Key to Success: The Follow-Through! Announce some easy-fix victories right there at the event. Then, have a clear system to track what was brought up and the progress being made on longer-term irritants. Without action, the next roast will be even more brutal (and rightfully so!).

The Empowerment SWAT Team

- The Concept: Form a small, agile team specifically tasked with busting bureaucratic obstacles FAST. Employees submit their infuriating process, outdated rule, or whatever's slowing them down. This team has authority to implement immediate fixes, bypassing usual red tape.

- Why it Works: Shows action, not just talk. Plus, it taps into that desire to demolish something frustrating (in a productive way!). Could even become a bit of a competition – who uncovers the most ridiculous time-wasting hurdles?

Reverse Mentorship Required

- The Concept: Pair senior leaders with a junior employee who teaches them a skill essential to the company's future. Could be deciphering social media trends, mastering a new software, or understanding a key client demographic.
- Why it Works: Breaks hierarchy in a positive way. Leaders gain respect for skills they lack, and the younger staff member builds confidence. Plus, it combats that "out of touch" feeling that often leads to disengagement.

"If I Ran the Zoo" Workshop

- The Concept: Give teams free reign to reimagine their department, project, or workflow with zero initial limitations. They present their bold vision, then leadership works BACKWARDS from that ideal to what's attainable, maybe even in small phases.
- Why it Works: Taps into the hidden brilliance that gets squashed by "reality" too soon. Often, even unfeasible ideas contain a nugget of something that could be truly

improved. Shows people you're serious about fresh thinking.

The Complaint Department (With a Twist)

- The Concept: Designate a time and space for pure, unfiltered venting about the change process. BUT, here's the key: Each gripe MUST be accompanied with a proposed solution, no matter how outlandish initially.

- Why it Works: Separates productive criticism from whiny defeatism. People feel heard, and it forces them to shift from "it sucks" to "what might actually make it better?" Leadership gets valuable insights, even buried within the rants.

COMMON CHALLENGES and OUR REMEDIES

Poor Change Communication: The Corporate Mumble: Are company updates written in code only robots understand? Cut the jargon and focus on WHY decisions matter, not just announcing the change itself.

- **Ask, Don't Just Tell**: One-way communication is a morale killer. Create easy ways for people to ask questions, offer alternatives, even voice frustrations. Ignoring that chatter isn't strength, it's a ticking time bomb.

Siloed Organization: Collaboration Killer

Turf Wars and Knowledge Hoarders Kill Good Ideas: Does each department think they're defending a medieval castle, not part of the same damn team? Are there a few star players everyone relies on, creating bottlenecks?

- Force collaboration through mixed team projects focused on those nagging company-wide problems.
- Knowledge Sharing, Not Hoarding: Make the star players share what they know. Mentoring less experienced folks upskills everyone and spreads the essential info around.

Managers' Dilemma

- Stuck in the Squeeze: Managers often take the most heat during change. Do they have a safe space to vent to their higher-ups? Or does every exchange end with more tasks unloaded onto their buried desks?
- Give 'Em the Masterplan: Training on the how is great if the why is clear!: Understanding where all this chaos is heading enables managers to better communicate the why to their exhausted teams.

No pauses Allowed!

- The Never-ending To-Do List: Prioritization is key! If everything is "urgent" nothing is. Have the guts to pause or kill lower-impact projects temporarily to free up bandwidth for the truly transformative tasks.
- Celebrate the Boring: Once a big change is implemented, pause to give people time to MASTER it before throwing the next curveball. Competence breeds

confidence, which is essential for tackling further change down the road.

"Busy" is the Enemy of Progress: Are people working long hours on meaningless tasks? Scrutinize inefficient processes, pointless meetings, and that creeping scope that turns every project into a monster.

- Time for WHAT Matters: Can you temporarily pull star players from routine work to focus solely on transformation initiatives? Sometimes clearing the decks enables real headway.

 Grab Your Compass!

Worksheets

Enablement

Enablement

Worksheet E1: The "And You Thought YOUR Day Was Bad" Exchange

Objective: To understand the struggles hiding behind the facade of workplace perfection.

Materials Needed: A deck of prompt cards (see examples below!), a timer, comfy seating arranged for easy sharing.

Steps:

- Warm-Up: Leader sets the tone: "We all have those days that make you want to crawl back into bed. But, we rarely share them beyond a vague grumble. Today gets real."

- The Shuffle & Share: Each person draws, facing away from the group. They have 2 minutes to share a recent moment that fits the prompt, however serious or silly.

- Empathy, Not Solutions: Listeners just hear – no advice, comments, just acknowledgement of the struggle.

Prompt Card Examples:

- "The time I almost cried at work but played it off as allergies…"
- "My most ridiculous commute nightmare…"
- "A client/coworker comment that still makes me cringe…"
- "My most embarrassing tech fail (and how I recovered)…"

Reflection: Was it harder to share those 'unprofessional' moments than you expected? Did hearing others' struggles change your perception of anyone on the team?

Enablement

Worksheet E2: The "Walk a Mile in My Work Boots" Challenge

Objective:

To gain a deeper understanding of and respect for the challenges faced in different roles within the company.

Materials Needed:

Pre-arranged "job shadowing" opportunities, a list of guiding questions (see below), time for reflection at the end.

Steps:

- The Pairs: Match people up who likely interact minimally in their usual work. Tech wizard gets paired with a customer service rep on the frontlines, the accountant shadows someone in creative...

- Not Just Observing, Doing: They spend an hour (or more if feasible) trying to perform basic tasks in their partner's area – answering irate calls, deciphering code, etc. They're instructed NOT to complain, just try.

- Guided Debrief: Questions like: What was most surprising? What skill do you have newfound respect for? What's ONE thing that could be changed to make your partner's job easier?

Reflection: Did this alter your assumptions about certain roles? Can any of those "one thing" suggestions be implemented quickly for a tangible win?

Enablement

Worksheet E3: The "You Don't Know Me (Yet)" Reveal

Objective:

To challenge assumptions and build connections based on shared experiences, not just job titles.

Materials Needed:

Index cards, pens, and an open space for the big reveal.

Steps:

- Anonymous Reflections: Everyone writes 3 things on their cards: 1) A past struggle that shaped them 2) A passion outside of work that brings them joy 3) Hidden skill no one would suspect they possess.

- The Gallery Shuffle: Cards get posted on the wall. People circulate, reading without comments or revealing who wrote what.

- Guess Who: Each person picks the card they find most fascinating and try to guess who in the group wrote it and why they chose those reveals.

- The "Aha!": Time for writers to announce their card(s) and elaborate if they wish.

Reflection:

Were you surprised by anyone's reveals? Do you feel potential new connections based on shared experiences, not just org chart hierarchy?

Enablement

Worksheet E4: The "Help Me, Help You" Exchange

Objective:

To move from passive support to truly understanding the kind of help that's useful during times of stress or change.

Materials Needed:

"Help Type" prompt cards (see below), space to mingle as pairs, sticky notes for post-it feedback.

Steps:

- My Way or the Highway: Leader explains that 'support' is very individual, what's helpful for one person could be annoying to another.

- Pick Your Type: Each person draws a card, keeping it private. The cards have things like: Direct Problem Solver, Empathetic Listener, Distraction Enthusiast, "Leave Me Alone" Type.

- Pair & Roleplay: People mingle, finding a partner. Each shares a current stressor (work focused), then reveals their "help type." The partner tries to support them in that style, however unnatural it feels.

- Honest Feedback: Sticky notes are the key! Partners give each other feedback – what did and DID NOT feel helpful, even if their type is the opposite.

Reflection:

Is your default 'help mode' what those around you actually need? How can you be more intentional about the kind of support you offer team members?

Case Study

Unleashing Potential at Frontline Retail – How One Company Ditched Demotivating Rules to Empower Their Team

The Challenge: Horizon Sales was a mid-sized retailer of sporting goods with a classic problem: they knew their frontline employees were the key to exceptional customer experiences, yet those employees felt undervalued, micromanaged, and burnt out. Turnover was high, especially among their most enthusiastic new hires, and morale was dismal despite attempts at generic "Employee Appreciation" events. This wasn't just impacting their bottom line but also their ability to adapt as e-commerce began stealing market share. Horizon's leadership realized a shift was urgently needed; they couldn't just offer better prices; they needed a stellar in-store experience to remain competitive.

The "Enablement" Revolution

Instead of the usual jargon-filled pronouncements about a new focus on "empowerment," Horizon made it clear this was going to be about action, not posters. Here's how they tackled those core obstacles that get in the way of teams truly owning their work:

Busting Bureaucratic Bottlenecks

- Death to the Dress Code: Their outdated uniform policy was more suited for 1950s office drones than a team selling activewear. They replaced it with broad guidelines (brand colors, safety-focused), and let individuals express themselves within those. The impact was immediate – employees felt more comfortable, which translated to confidence when interacting with customers.
- "Power to the Pricing Guns": Employees were given the authority to offer small discounts on the spot to close a sale, resolve minor customer complaints, or price match within set parameters. This eliminated the need to escalate every little thing to a manager, speeding up transactions and making employees feel trusted.

Growth Beyond Job Titles

- Mastering Their Domain: Horizon invested in product-specific training, turning staff into mini-experts. A runner wasn't just stocking shoes but could advise on the best fit for terrain and customer goals. This fueled enthusiasm, and those product deep-dives frequently led to increased upsells.
- Sharing the Knowledge: Instead of relying solely on outside trainers, they implemented a mentorship

system. The veteran hiking enthusiast trained up newbies on gear; the tech-savvy teen helped older staff finally master the inventory system. This built camaraderie across experience levels.

Ditching Demotivating Systems

- Scheduling Sanity: Instead of auto-generated shifts, managers were required to have 1:1 conversations about schedule preferences. Balancing part-timer availability with peak hours remained a challenge, but incorporating input boosted morale and decreased "no call, no show" absences.
- Time Theft…From Themselves: Mandatory unpaid meetings before/after shifts were axed. Key info was delivered in short huddles at shift changeover, minimizing the feeling that their personal time wasn't valued.

Making the Work…Work BETTER

- "Suggestion Box" Revamp: The dusty box was replaced with a dedicated Slack channel. But here's the key…a team of rotating volunteers was responsible for triaging the complaints, escalating those truly fixable, and publicly responding (even when the answer was 'no'). This showed that feedback was taken seriously.
- Tech Tools that Don't Suck: They finally admitted their glitchy point-of-sale system was costing them in lost sales and employee frustration. Investing in a

streamlined UI with dedicated training time had a surprisingly swift impact on productivity and stress levels at checkout.

How this Played out in Specific Roles

Role #1: Sales Floor Staff

Challenges:

- Feeling Like Robots: Scripted sales pitches and pressure to upsell at all costs kill enthusiasm and lead to inauthentic customer interactions.

- Knowledge = Power...But They Lack It: Without in-depth product knowledge, they're just cashiers, not the brand ambassadors they could be.

- The Hamster Wheel: Repetitive tasks, long shifts on their feet, and cranky customers lead to rapid burnout.

Empowering Actions:

- Own the Conversation: Training focused on identifying genuine customer needs, ditching the memorized spiels. Confidence in suggesting the RIGHT product, not just the most expensive one, builds trust.

- Product Masterclasses: Those deep-dives on features, benefits, even how to demo items in a way that gets customers excited. Turn them into mini-experts.

- A Little Autonomy Goes a Long Way: Let them tweak displays, champion products they believe in, experiment with how they engage shoppers. This combats the feeling of being a replaceable cog in the machine.

Role #2: Stockroom & Inventory Specialists

Challenges:

- The Unseen Force: They're essential, but often feel like the bottom of the totem pole. Customer interactions are rare, making recognition scarce.
- Tech from the Dark Ages: Outdated inventory systems, illegible picking lists, and constant mismatches between what's "in stock" digitally vs. reality makes their job unnecessarily difficult.
- Process Bottlenecks: They see how a simple rule change could speed things up but have no way to communicate those inefficiencies to anyone who can act on them.

Empowering Actions:

- Spotlight Those Wins: Quantify the impact of their work! Was there a sales spike due to ensuring hot items were quickly replenished? Showcase that data.
- Upgrade Their Arsenal: Even if a complete system overhaul is not feasible, are there small tech improvements or even crowd-sourced hacks that could improve workflows? Involve them in finding solutions.
- Direct Line to Decision-Makers: Regular "Stockroom Summits" where they directly present those pain points

that slow everything down, cutting through the hierarchy.

Role #3: Store Management

Challenges:

- Stuck in the Middle: Pressure from higher-ups is relentless, but their ability to make meaningful changes for their team is often limited. This leads to cynicism and makes them ineffective advocates for those they manage.
- Data Dumps, No Direction: Corporate sends sales figures and vague pronouncements on "improving morale," but lacks support to enact real change.
- Putting Out Fires: Understaffing and constant troubleshooting leaves little time for the leadership that would boost their team's long-term success.

Empowering Actions:

- The "Why" Behind the What: Don't make them just the enforcers of change, loop them in on strategy discussions. Understanding the bigger picture lets them tailor communication in a way their team trusts.
- Own Your Zone: Give them increased budget flexibility and decision-making power (even in seemingly small ways) to address store-specific obstacles. This builds their authority.

- Mandatory Mentorship: Pair them with a successful manager at another location. This peer learning is more actionable than generic leadership seminars.

Important Caveat: Store culture matters! Even well-intentioned "enablement" efforts will fail if the overall environment is toxic or trust between leadership and frontline staff has severely eroded. You may need to win some small, trust-building victories before tackling bigger systemic changes.

The Results that Mattered:

- Sales Success, From the Source: Customer surveys started coming back with specific praise for knowledgeable and helpful staff. Those product "deep dive" trainings paid off, with employees confidently steering customers towards purchases they truly valued.

- Problem-Solvers, Not Order Takers: With the ability to make those small judgment calls, both customers and employees felt more empowered. Complaint resolution became about crafting solutions on the spot, not just apologizing and passing the buck.

- Pride in the Place: As turnover decreased and a team identity formed, something unexpected occurred – the store itself became better cared for. Displays were more creative; stockroom organization improved without nagging from above. This had a direct impact on the customer experience, even without pricey store redesigns.

- Adapting to the Unexpected: When a sudden supply chain issue hit, the team's problem-solving skills weren't limited to irate customers. They brainstormed alternative product displays, came up with creative in-store events to keep the buzz going, and their improved communication systems allowed for quick pivots as the situation changed.

Key Takeaway:

In retail, customer focus is king. But Horizon learned a valuable lesson: you can't have exceptional customer experiences with a demoralized and restricted team. Their "enablement" focused on removing demoralizing obstacles, providing actionable ways to grow, and demonstrating through action that employee voices truly mattered. This translated directly into a team equipped and motivated to make Horizon worthy of customer loyalty, even amidst a volatile retail landscape.

Enablement

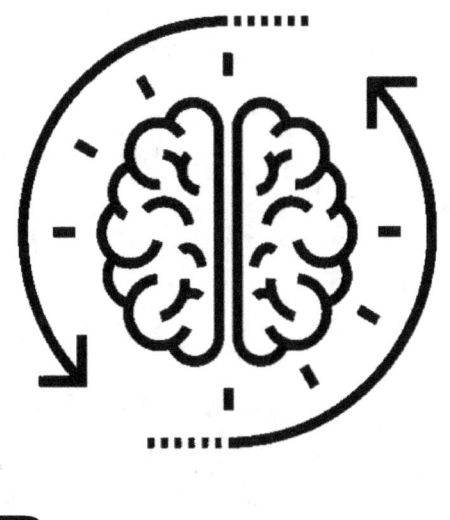

REFLECTION

Pauses to Power Up Your Brain

Why Is Practicing Reflection Critical to Employee Engagement?

Reflection helps employees pause to learn from their work. Today it is a new leadership meta skill to gain insights and improve. It also forces a pause from the onslaught of urgent requests and constant change to help build resilience. A culture of reflection engages employees in frequent constructive feedback. It enables everyone to focus and to recognize and appreciate individual and team contributions.

One study found **37% of employees** feel most encouraged by feedback offering positive personal recognition. And if recruiter Zippia's research is correct,

- **79% of employees leave** because they don't feel appreciated by leaders and
- **69% percent** believe they'd work harder if their work was recognized.

Reflection and practical experience are powerful partners! Once an employee reaches a certain level of experience, reflection can be more beneficial than more experience. Sometimes reflection trumps experience!

- Studies show reflecting on feedback and learnings can increase performance **as much as 23%**.
- Get this! Studies also show reflection can reduce stress and enhance well-being.

While writing this book, we often got stuck on how best to share a particular practice with you. Often one of us woke up with a new and viable solution. Have you experienced this too? Sleep is often the pause that boosts creativity. It surprises us with new connections that were not obvious to us while we were awake.

> Edison had a favorite chair for what we like to call his innovation naps. He carefully staged his naps to capture new ideas. Before his nap, Edison placed a metal bowl

beside his favorite chair so that his hand holding a metal ball hung directly over it. When he entered REM sleep, his muscles relaxed, and his hand released the metal ball - which hit the metal pan with a loud clang! He promptly woke up to write down the new solutions he had discovered during his sleep – yes, he kept writing supplies handy for this purpose. In REM sleep, Edison's brain connected the new information he was exploring before his nap to already existing information stored in his brain. Your brain does this too!

Tip: Keep a notebook or mobile near your bed to capture new and prescient ideas that come to you in your sleep!

Alright, let's dump the textbook vibe and make this about integrating moments of meaningful reflection into the workday (because who hasn't zoned out during a mandatory journaling session?).

KEY OUTCOME

We're not just cogs in the machine cranking out tasks; we're self-reflective dynamos who use our strengths, learn from our weaknesses, and practice the art of bouncing back even in our sleep! Our individual and shared reflection practices build resilience to enable us to navigate the obstacle course of change.

How to Model Reflection:

If you roll your eyes at "reflective practices", this is what your teams see, and no amount of backtracking can erase this momentary negative feedback from you. Our expressions and body language are never lost on any audience!

Reflection promises to increase engagement when you practice it yourself and make it visible. Don't worry, your excitement about your own outcomes will inspire your teams!

- The Walk, Not Just the Talk: Make sure you visibly engage in reflection and connect those insights to decisions made and problems solved. Try Worksheet R2.

- Share the Struggle (a Little): It's powerful when leaders admit, "I thought that strategy was solid, but here's why it didn't work as intended and what I'm doing differently because of it." This shows reflection is for everyone, and it also models vulnerability. Yes, most of the CLOVER practices reinforce each other! Try Workbook R1 and tie it to your Vulnerability Practice.

- Shift to Frequent Reflection Check-ins: Those annual performance review sit-downs are often demoralizing for team members and their managers. Shift to more frequent check-ins with a heavy dose of two-way reflection. Not just "hit your KPIs or else!" but "where are you feeling stuck and how can I help" or "where are you feeling proud and how can we celebrate this achievement"? Try Worksheet R1.

Reflection

How to Coach Reflection:

We get it – sometimes, the pace of change feels like being trapped on a runaway train. Reflection isn't about wasting time; it's about tuning in and tuning up to regain a little sanity amidst the chaos. Reflection exercises help you coach your teams to truly learn and reconnect with the higher purpose of the enterprise. You can train them to take energy from the whirlwind of change. Let's practice our resilience muscles to help us bounce back together.

Want to Pause Now and Jump Start Your Reflection Practice? Go to Worksheet R1 and take the first step: schedule your first Reflection Hour with your teams. While you are waiting for this event on your calendar, keep reading to learn about your important role as a reflection coach and how to navigate some pitfalls you might encounter.

For those of you who paused to schedule your first Reflection Hour with your teams, Welcome Back!

KEY ACTIONS: Your Reflective Coaching Playbook

Make "Think Time" Sacred

- The Meeting Purge: Could some of those routine meetings be ruthlessly cut to free up time for actual reflection? Take an honest look at your calendar bloat! Your teams will applaud! Try Worksheet R7.
- End of Project Rituals: Build in a mandatory pause after a project wraps (even if deadlines were tight). A focused

debrief on successes AND failures is how teams get better, not just busier. Try Worksheet R6.

- "Focus Fridays" (or Whatever Works): Can you carve out even a half-day per week where individual reflection time is protected? No endless meetings, batch those emails – give brains the space to actually process what's been happening.

Focus on What Can Make Me Smarter Next Time!

- Forget the Journal. Unless They Love It: Forcing everyone into the same mold usually fails. Offer a variety of tools: voice memos, guided prompts, even art supplies for those who think visually.

- Solitude vs. Sharing: Some folks need quiet alone time to reflect meaningfully. Others thrive when bouncing ideas off colleagues. Create spaces and time for both approaches. For any activity or worksheet, first allot some quiet time to brainstorm using stickies. Then ask folks to share their ideas.

- Tie It to Action, Not Abstracts: Don't make reflection about just chronicling your feelings. Frame it as essential prep for the next challenge: "What do I know now, because of this experience, that will make me smarter next time?" Try Workshop R2.

Focus on the Feelings (Yeah, We're Going There)

- Beyond Happy/Sad: A simple "feelings wheel" can help people articulate deeper emotions that impact work. Sometimes, lingering frustration or unrecognized pride needs to be acknowledged before true forward progress happens.

- Feedback as Fuel: Train everyone (leaders especially!) in giving constructive, specific feedback. Reflection is pointless if it's only fueled by self-critique and never gets that outside perspective.

- Burnout Isn't Badass, it's a Problem: Make it clear that reflection includes being honest about mental exhaustion levels. Waiting until someone spectacularly flames out is a failure. Proactive stress reduction strategies are key! Introduce this topic using Worksheet R1.

Target Your Reflective Firepower

- Prioritized Reflections: Focus those in-depth, soul-searching reflection sessions strategically. New hires with onboarding questions, those tackling challenging projects, etc., get priority.

- Team Dynamics Matter: Is there a particularly dysfunctional team where honest reflection could be a game-changer? Use skilled facilitation to prioritize interventions tailored to them without enabling another gripe-fest.

- "Win Skeptics" Strategy: Sometimes those most resistant to reflection become believers when it leads to tangible improvements that directly benefits them. Find those quick win opportunities! More to come in **How to Rescue a Flailing Reflection Practice.**

How to Reward Reflection: WIIFM

SOMETIMES FOLKS NEED A NUDGE! Are you with us?

Sometimes you gotta nudge folks towards a good habit, especially when the benefits of reflection aren't obvious to everyone. Let's tackle how to motivate without resorting to raffles & retreats.

Incentives, Done Right: Recognize Wins in the Reflection Knowledge Hub (Worksheet R6)

- Focus on the WHY: Don't just announce "reflection time!" Make it tangible: "Invest 30 minutes in reflecting on how to streamline [that annoying process everyone hates], and your insights might lead to actual change, saving everyone hours each week..." Specificity beats vagueness! Try Worksheet R2.

- "Wins" Are Currency: Was there a particularly insightful team debrief that led to a smarter way of working? Reward that team with a perk – priority scheduling for a hot new tool, a "skip one pointless meeting" pass, or even just bragging rights at the company all-hands. Try Worksheet R6.

- Make It a Competition (The Healthy Kind): Can you gamify some reflection? Teams compete for the "Most Outrageously Useful Failure Analysis", the "Best Prediction of Future Obstacles", etc. Keep prizes lighthearted, focus on the playful rivalry. Try Worksheet R4 and R2.

- The Power of Peer Recognition: Implement a system where anyone can give a virtual shoutout to a teammate for thoughtful reflection or their particularly helpful feedback during a meeting. Tie these to small, desirable rewards (extra break time, choosing the theme for casual Friday...). When recognition comes from peers, not just on high, it has more impact. Try Worksheet R1.

Incentives to Handle With Caution:

- Individual Bribes Backfire: Paying people to fill out a reflection worksheet just breeds resentment. Make the reward the outcome (your insights led to a better workflow!), not the act of going through the motions. Try Worksheet R1.

- Public Leaderboards = Anxiety: Ranking people on how "reflective" they seem creates a toxic culture. Focus on celebrating team successes fueled by reflection, not making individuals feel compared or inadequate. Try Worksheet R6 instead!

- Avoid the "Feel Good" Trap: If the only outcome of reflection is vaguely positive affirmations, it becomes pointless. Incentivize that connection between reflection and acting – that's what makes it powerful! Try Worksheet R5.

How to Celebrate Reflection Wins:

Frequently there are moments when a project almost tanks or a mistake is made and quickly glossed over. Celebrating the near misses and reflecting about them will help you get the most out of your own and your teams' reflection practices over time. This extra step will cement the connection between reflection and impact.

- **Celebrate the "AHA!" Not Just the Wins**: Sure, analyze why that project succeeded, but spend equal time picking apart the near-misses. The real learning goldmine is often found in what ALMOST worked. Use Worksheet R1 with the AHA theme.

- **Share (Some of) the Learnings**: Create a knowledge hub where key takeaways from reflection sessions are accessible. This prevents the same mistakes from being repeated and shows people their reflections have worth beyond the moment. Use Worksheet R6 to share the learnings. Make sure you track Near Misses (above) and Trendlines (below) in your the Knowledge hub.

- **Track the Trendlines, Not Just the Drama:** Can you quantify the impact of reflection over time? Decreased time wasted repeating the same errors, smoother project launches due to anticipating obstacles learned from past reflection... hard data wins over skeptics. Track Trendlines in your Knowledge Hub and make the trends visible using Worksheet R6.

How to Sustain Your Reflection Practice:

The Long Game: Reflection Gains that Last!

Ultimately, the best incentive is showing that sustained reflection makes a difference. Here's where leadership plays a crucial role:

- **Continue to Walk the Walk**: When a leader frequently and publicly changes course because of insights gained during reflection, it sends a powerful message. Add your personal stories to the knowledge hub and share them during the next Reflection Activity.

- **Close the Loop**: If a team brainstorms brilliant improvements during reflection time, make sure those get implemented (or at least there's a transparent explanation of why not right now). Nothing kills enthusiasm faster than feeling your reflections vanish into the void. Capture it in the Knowledge Hub and point it out at your next reflection hour (Worksheet R1 or R6) with the team!

- **Cultivate Reflective Champions**: Those naturally introspective folks? Enlist them! Their genuine enthusiasm for the process becomes contagious and is far more effective with their peers than a corporate HR initiative. Try naming Reflective Champions in Worksheets R3 and R4.

- **Early Wins**: Sometimes even long-lasting and well-intentioned incentives can feel manipulative, especially if your company culture is historically distrustful. Start with voluntary "reflection pilots" on teams where there's already some trust. Their wins will pave the way for wider acceptance. Example: Pilot Worksheets R1 – R3. Reflect. Pilot Worksheets R4 – R6.

Turn Familiar Pains into Gains

Gain #1: Communication Champions Resolve Lack of Communication

- The "Unsung Hero" Award: Combat that feeling that good work goes unnoticed. Teams nominate a member whose behind-the-scenes contributions to smooth communication were essential. Focus on the specific impact, not just vague praise. Worksheets R1 and R6 may help!

- "Train the Translator" Challenge: Is miscommunication often due to tech folks and creatives speaking different languages? Incentivize cross-team pairings where they reflect together on a recent stumble and create a mini "cheat sheet" to improve understanding. The reward is less frustration in the future! Add the checklist to the Knowledge Hub and review it using Worksheet R6.

GAIN #2: Collaboration Resolves Siloed Problem Solving

- "Speed Dating" for Problem-Solving: Facilitate quick round-robin sessions where different departments bring their current roadblock. Others offer solutions wildly outside their usual domain. Reward the most surprisingly helpful idea, proving the benefit of fresh perspectives. Try Worksheet R4 to collect and brainstorm roadblocks. Use Worksheet R6 to reward fresh perspectives.

- The "Walk a Mile" Reflection: Incentivize job shadowing with a twist. The focus isn't just on learning the tasks, but reflecting on WHY those tasks are done that way. The outsider's insights are often eye-opening, and the reward could be that "shadower" having some influence on streamlining the process. Does Worksheet R2 or R4 help you here?

Turn Disengaged Managers into Empowered Managers

- "Vent + Vision" Sessions: Give your middle managers a safe space to air frustrations, followed by guided reflection on what THEY can control even within constraints. Small wins are sometimes all it takes to shift from feeling helpless to empowered... which benefits their whole team. Try Worksheet R1.

- Reverse Mentoring Required: Pair them with a junior employee for a focused reflection session on a recent tech change or communication style shift. Learning from those who are thriving amidst the chaos can be humbling (in a good way!) and combats that "out of touch" feeling.

Celebration and Humor can Refresh Change Fatigue

- The "Celebrate the Pause" Project: When a big initiative is completed, incentivize taking time to truly explore what worked before immediately launching the next thing. The reward could be some control over the pacing of future projects, since they proved the value of a "sanity gap." Try Worksheet R6.

- "Change Mascots": This one gets silly! Have teams choose a ridiculous mascot to represent a past arduous change. The reflection centers on lessons learned told through the "mascot's" perspective. Humor breaks down the wall of exhaustion. Use your newly named Change Mascot in all of your reflection activities when change seems arduous.

Expand Focus Time to Resolve the "Too Busy" Syndrome

- Micro-Reflection Missions: Can you incentivize those 2-minute bursts of reflection at the end of a task or meeting? The "One Win, One Obstacle" prompt forces a quick analysis. Aggregate these insights to reveal major time-wasters. Add them to the Knowledge Hub.

- Meeting Massacre Bounty: Track time spent in pointless meetings for a week. Then, put a bounty on identifying the most egregious ones. Those who successfully argue to kill a recurring time-sponge are rewarded with time BACK for focused work.

Never underestimate the power of non-material rewards! Sometimes, a bit of targeted autonomy, the chance to impact a decision, or even getting to ditch a dumb, hated task is far more motivating than another coffee mug.

How to Rescue a Floundering Reflection Practice

Reflection

We have 60 years of cumulative experience coaching hundreds of teams to reflect! We hope to help you prepare for some of the reactions you may encounter when you ask you teams to pause and reflect.

What is the #1 pitfall we encountered when coaching teams to reflect? Here it is!

#1 Pitfall: ONE SIZE FITS ALL

Let's figure out how to make reflection resonate with the diverse personalities you'll encounter on any team. One size definitely does NOT fit all when it comes to digging a little deeper!

Step 1: Brainstorm the Stereotypes (a little tongue-in-cheek, of course!) Do you recognize them on your teams?

- The Over-Sharer: They'll happily dissect their emotional state in the middle of the team meeting. Channeling this enthusiasm is key, without it feeling like therapy hour

- The Stoic Analyst: Emotions? Never heard of them. But they're meticulous about tracking their progress and setbacks. Find ways to help them see the value of going beyond just the data of what happened.

- The "Too Busy to Think": Always rushing, every conversation is transactional. For them, micro-reflection moments might be the only way in.

- The Eternal Sceptic: Forced "positivity" makes them roll their eyes. Reflection only gains their respect when it's ruthlessly focused on problem-solving.

Step 2: Choose Your Battles, Find Your Easy Win!

You won't transform everyone overnight, so prioritize! Focus on those who are naturally a bit more introspective or those in roles where reflection can have the biggest immediate impact on the team dynamic. Their successful reflection stories become a better motivator than any mandated exercise.

Step 3: Tailor Reflection Techniques for the Stereotypes You Identified in Step 1:

- The Over-Sharer:
    - Channel the Chatter: Ask them to be a "Reflection Buddy" to others who struggle with being vulnerable. They can meet for short, informal debriefs after projects, keeping it focused on takeaways.
    - Private But Purposeful: A simple 1:1 with their manager focused on what they LEARNED from their emotional response to a situation can be valuable without being intrusive.

- The Stoic Analyst:
    - Data + Deeper Questions: They love their stats, but ask "Why do you think that pattern is occurring?" This encourages them to analyze the process, not just the outcome.
    - The "What If" Scenario: Present them with hypothetical challenges based on past projects. Their solutions will reveal potential blind spots to reflect on further.

- The "Too Busy to Think"

    o Tiny Timeouts: 2 mins at the end of a meeting – "One thing that went unexpectedly right today? One roadblock we keep hitting?" Plant the seed.

    o Voice Memo Moments: If writing feels like a chore, let them record short reflections on the go. This captures the 'in the moment' insight better than a retrospective analysis.

- The Eternal Sceptic

    o No Nonsense Zone: Skip the warm-fuzzies, frame reflection as a competitive advantage. "What's ONE thing the competition does better, and how do we analyze why?"

    o Blunt Feedback is Best: They respect directness. Make their reflection sessions focus on how their actions impact team outcomes (positively and negatively).

Keep in mind: Company culture matters! If cynicism runs deep, start with small wins in safe spaces. Even the most resistant types are swayed when they see these reflection practices actually lead to better outcomes.

Step 4: Did you discover some change-resistant types on your teams? Let's not forget these 2:

Reflection

Ah, yes, those classic change-resistant archetypes! Let's strategize ways to break through their negativity and get them to see the potential value in reflection, even if they never become enthusiastic cheerleaders of the process.

Confronting the "Naysayer"

- Their Core Complaint: Everything is pointless, change sucks, focusing on problems makes things worse... blah, blah, blah.

- Reflection Reframe: Focus on solutions, not whining. Shift their role to "Chief Obstacle Identifier." Have them meticulously list out every potential problem with an upcoming project – force them to go beyond their usual vague doom-and-gloom pronouncements.

- The Power of Prediction: By articulating problems in advance, two things happen: 1) Some of those roadblocks might get mitigated early on 2) When the project DOES succeed (even partially), their focus on the negative makes the win even sweeter.

Confronting the "Know-It-All"

- Their Core Complaint: They have all the answers, their experience makes them superior, any analysis is beneath them. Ouch.

- Reflection Reframe: Turn them into a "Mentor on Steroids." Pair them with someone less experienced. The task? Reflect with their mentee on a recent success AND a failure. Force them to articulate why things worked or didn't – this act of teaching deepens their own understanding.

- "Reverse Nostalgia": Instead of their usual "back in my day" rants, challenge them: "In 5 years, when you're looking back on this transformation, what will make you feel PROUD we accomplished that others might have thought impossible?"

Step 5: Bonus Tactics for Most Archetypes:

- The "Prove It" Challenge: Don't just tell them reflection works, show them. Did a team they respect try it with success? Share that case study (anonymized if needed). Exploring the possible with a few competitive streaks can be useful!

- Go Granular: Open-ended "reflect on your feelings" prompts are useless. Focus on hyper-specific micro-tasks: "What was the most efficient part of your work today, and can you replicate it?" Tiny wins lower defences.

- Leader Leverage: Is there a well-respected manager these folks DO listen to, even a bit? Get them on board. A nudge from someone they trust is far more effective than company-wide pronouncements.

Important Caveat: Sometimes stereotypical reactions mask real issues. "This is a waste of time" might be code for "my ideas are never heard!" Finding ways to engage these folks in solution-finding activities with actionable take-aways, alongside a bit of structured reflection, could make them surprising allies down the line.

 Grab Your Compass!

 Hit The Pause Button!

BONUS SECTION
OUR **REFLECTIONS** ON THE HARD WORK OF CHANGE

Why Taking a Brain Break Might Just Save Your (and your team's) Sanity

Change is the only constant, right? Whether it's that "exciting" new software that makes you want to chuck your laptop, or a company re-org that leaves everyone wondering who to report to... sometimes it feels like we barely survive the chaos, let alone excel amidst it. Change fatigue is real, but hold on – there's a secret weapon that might help you and your teams bounce back! Hit the pause button for a little thing called reflection.

No, we're not talking about spa days and meditation retreats (though they're awesome if you can swing it). This is about making time to dissect your work, dig into what's working, name a dumpster fire, and ask why. Think of it as taking a pit stop during a marathon to adjust your shoes, so you don't end up limping across the finish line with blisters and a bad attitude.

Why Reflection Is for Bouncing Back – Not Navel Gazing!

- Skip the Drama, Get Results: Whining about problems feels good for about five seconds, then you're still stuck with the problems. Reflection forces you to shift from "this is a disaster!" to "how can we fix this, and what's my role in making that happen?"

- Know Thyself (Even the Cranky Parts): Turns out, most of us aren't robots who can just shut off emotions at work. Reflecting on how you're feeling – frustrated, secretly proud, creatively blocked, bored – can pinpoint the root of why you're struggling... or excelling.

- Become a Self-Improvement Ninja: Instead of mindlessly repeating the same mistakes, reflection lets you learn the "why" behind them. This isn't about beating yourself up; it's about spotting patterns to work smarter, not just harder. And to share your learnings to help others.

- Upgrade Your Hogwash Detector: Ever get told a change is happening "because that's the way we've always done it"? Reflection helps you call Hogwash on outdated processes or recognize "fear of the unfamiliar" is holding everyone back.

- Empathy = Power: Taking a step back to reflect on your teammates' struggles, or how your actions impact clients, makes you way better at your job. It's not a show of weakness but harnesses your strengths for strategic problem-solving with a systems view.

Okay, But When Do I Have **TIME** for This Soul-Searching Stuff?

We get it – you're drowning in to-do lists and this reminds you a bit of inspirational self-help posters. Here's the deal: pausing to reflect **saves time** as you integrate shared learnings into how you work.

- Micro-Moments Matter: Five minutes at the end of a project to jot down what went surprisingly right, and one obstacle to avoid next time... that's a valuable reflection practice. Can you 12x the value of your effort? Share it to help a teammate or your whole team. Now it saves time at a systems level.

- Make Meetings Count (or Kill Them): Explore your calendar bloat. Could some of those boring status updates be replaced with a quick hit list of wins and roadblocks? Now we are reflecting on our progress instead of staring for a miserable hour at PowerPoints that are already out-of date. See Worksheet R7

- Leaders, Lead the Way: If bosses only 'reflect' when there's a crisis, forget it. Make sharing those small lessons learned (good AND bad) a part of "how we work at our company".

The Real Reasons Reflection Rocks + Why Some Folks Still Hate It

1. It Exposes What Needs Fixin': Bad processes, pointless policies, that one coworker who derails everything... reflection shines a harsh light on stuff that's gotta change. And, yeah, sometimes that gets uncomfortable.

2. Not Everyone Wants to Look in the Mirror: Some folks would rather blame everything external than admit they might need a new skill or (gasp!) a mindset shift. Can't force those types into the land of introspection overnight.

3. "Feel Good" Fluff is the WORST: Mandatory journaling about your emotions with no connection to how it improves you or your job? This breeds cynicism, not self-aware superstars.

Getting Started on Your Reflection Revolution:

- One Size Does NOT Fit All: Guided meditation makes you break out in hives? Fine! Maybe your reflection is ranting into a voice memo or sketching out a problem visually. Find what works for YOU.

- Team Up: Some people thrive on bouncing ideas off others, while some need solo quiet time. Offer both! Sharing those "Aha!" moments from reflection sessions builds momentum and makes it feel like a collective effort.

- Show, Don't Tell: Nobody buys into this until they see it leads to things getting better. Make the insights gained from reflection fuel improved processes, less burnout, and a sense that everyone's voice truly matters.

The Bottom Line:

Reflection helps you fine-tune your work (and your sanity!) amidst the chaos. Think of it as a power tool for the most important piece of equipment you own – your brain. Will it make you a Zen-Master? Probably not, unless you that becomes your next challenge!

FROM THINKING TO DOING:

Turning Those Brilliant Ideas into Actual Reality

Alright, you've embraced vulnerability, gotten real about your roadblocks, maybe even had a few lightbulb moments of "Wait, what if we did it THIS way instead?". But here's the thing about brilliant new ideas – they're worthless unless you can actually execute them. This section is dedicated to taking those sparks of change-fueled inspiration and turning them into the results that matter.

The Problem with "Good Intentions": Bridging the Gap between Thinking and Doing

We've all been there. That meeting brimming with excitement, the whiteboard covered in revolutionary plans... and then a month later, it's back to business as usual amidst the whirlwind of daily tasks. Change is hard!

Let's be honest – there's no magic formula to make change easy. But here are some strategies to combat those classic obstacles and increase your odds of those bright ideas actually seeing the light of day instead of fizzling out:

- "We Don't Have Time" Syndrome: Change needs dedicated time and resources. If it's always an afterthought tacked onto everyone's overflowing plate, progress crawls, or worse, never even begins. Try Worksheet R1.
- Call in the Demo Crew: Don't just talk about potential solutions, prototype them! Try a rough mock-up of a new workflow or a role-playing session to test-drive a new client interaction.

Stuck in Perfection Paralysis: Waiting for the flawless, everyone-agrees masterplan turns into a convenient excuse for inaction. Sometimes, a messy start is better than no start at all. Try Worksheet R2.

- The Accountability Void: Everyone nods enthusiastically when a new process is proposed, but who's actually responsible for making it happen? When ownership is vague, so is follow-through.

Name Names: Who is the "champion" of this initiative? They don't need to do all the work, but they own making sure progress happens.

Public accountability is surprisingly powerful! Resource Reallocation: Need to free up someone's time to focus on the change? Be clear about what gets deprioritized to make that happen. Good intentions don't pay the bills; strategic choices do.

Small Wins = Big Motivation: Break down that ambitious goal into bite-sized milestones. Celebrate each one visibly! This keeps spirits up when the end goal still feels a million miles away. Try Worksheet R3.

- The "Pre-Mortem" Experiment: Force teams to be brutally honest about why this initiative might fail. Addressing those potential pitfalls early on can make the execution far smoother. Fear of the Unknown: Even a much-needed change can be scary. Fear disguised as skepticism kills momentum. ("That'll never work because..."). Try Worksheet R4.

- Embrace Imperfect Pilots: Launch a "test and tweak" version of that new process. Gather real-world data quickly to prove what works and what needs fixing, without overplanning it. Try Worksheet R5.

- Track the Transformation: Have a visual reminder of the progress (even with setbacks!). A simple timeline with milestones reinforces the sense that this change isn't just talk, it's happening. Try Worksheet R3 or R4.

Dealing with the Change Deniers

Even with the best planning, there will be those who cling to the old ways, convinced any change is doomed. Address their resistance with powerful questions without getting dragged into negativity:

- The "Why Does It Matter Chatter": Instead of defending your brilliant plan, ask them; "If this problem remains unsolved, what's the consequence for you/your team/our clients?" Focus on the pain point they DO care about.

- Harness Their Pessimism: They're great at spotting potential failures! Channel that negative energy by asking; "How can we mitigate this risk?" Often, they have valuable insights, even if their delivery is less than inspiring.

- Invite, Don't Impose: Critiquing from afar is easy. Turn the distracting background noise into a bit of ownership by asking: "Can you be a part of the pilot project?" Often they are remaining on the fringe and don't know how to shift their perspective. Try Worksheet R3.

Remember, Sometimes Slow is Strategic:

Time is on your side! Not everyone needs to be an early adopter for change to be successful. Focus on getting those with influence onboard, and let the results eventually sway the stubborn holdouts.

- The Power of Progress Reports (That Aren't Boring) Chuck the Corporate-Speak: No one reads those 20-page updates full of jargon. Infographics, quick video snippets, even a "highlight reel" of small wins are far more impactful, especially for busy higher-ups. Use your Knowledge Hub for this!

- Own the Setbacks: Got off track? Don't sugarcoat it. Briefly state the problem, the course correction, and why you're confident it won't derail the whole project. Transparency builds trust. (Worksheet #4)

- Celebrate the "Unsung Heroes": Who went above and beyond to solve that unexpected glitch? Public recognition not only rewards those change-makers, it inspires others. Use your Knowledge Hub to capture recognition after acknowledging contributions in a public forum with the teams.

The Bottom Line: From "Aha!" to Outcomes

Turn those "Aha!" moments from workshops and reflection sessions into tangible outcomes that make everyone's work lives better – THAT'S the true test of whether transformation efforts are worth it. Stop chasing some abstract ideal of change and prove, one step at a time, that struggles lead to payoffs worth fighting for.

Worksheets

REFLECTION

Worksheet R1: The Reflection Hour

Objective

Designate a time for employees to reflect on their week's work, both the highs and the lows.

Materials Needed
Quiet space
Notebooks or digital note-taking tools

Steps

1. Schedule a specific hour each week for reflection.
2. Prepare optional questions to guide the reflection:
    - What was the highlight of your week?
    - What might you have done differently?
3. Model it to Coach it! Tell your own reflection story.
    1. How a reflection this week impacted/helped you
4. Ask team members to jot down their reflections

Reflection

- Recall how your reflection affected your engagement with your work and your colleagues (Step 3).
- Ask the team, "How did pausing to reflect affect your mindset, approach to work, and engagement levels?"

Worksheet R2: The "Make It Real" Mock-Up

Objective

Surface potential problems early and brainstorm creative fixes.

Steps

1. Keep it low-tech! This is NOT about polished presentations. Use whiteboard sketches, hand-drawn flowcharts, sticky notes... whatever gets the rough idea across quickly.
2. Choose a discussed new process, communication channel, or client-facing initiative that hasn't gained traction.
3. <u>Brainstorm the User Experience</u> Task everyone to think through the change from the perspective of those who'd be most impacted (employees, customers, etc.). Walk through each step as if YOU were the one using the new system.
4. Embrace Constructive Chaos: Get those creative juices flowing! Applaud poking holes, laughing at flawed elements, and brainstorming workarounds on the fly.

Reflection

- Did the act of prototyping reveal obstacles unseen in theoretical discussions?
- Which parts of the change seem surprisingly easy to implement after this visualization?
- Key Takeaway: Done is better than perfect, and a tangible start, even a messy one, often fuels better ideas than another round of planning.

Worksheet R3: The Accountability Assignment

Objective:

Clearly name owners and support roles to free a change initiative from the "everyone's responsible, so no one is" trap.

Steps:

1. Select a change initiative with potential solutions but no actions.
2. Name That Champion: Name a single person who is ultimately responsible for driving the change forward. The owner is the point person for progress: they do not do all the work.
3. The Support Squad: Name specific roles who can provide expertise, resources, or approval to make the change happen.
4. Timeline: Break the initiative into milestones with deadlines, even if tentative.

Reflection

- Was it harder than expected to agree on that "champion"? This exposes hidden hesitation about the idea itself.
- Are there resource gaps?
- Is the team promising support that they can realistically deliver without a shift in priorities?
- Is the timeline realistic?
- Key Takeaway: Accountability isn't about assigning blame, but about giving a good idea the structure it needs to succeed.

Reflection

Worksheet R4: The Pre-Mortem Panic Session

Objective:

Proactively brainstorm solutions to potential pitfalls that could derail a proposed change.

Steps:

1. Select a proposed change with buy-in and lurking fears about ways it could go sideways.

2. Assume Disaster: The project has crashed and burned. Task everyone to list ALL the reasons why, from the plausible to the outlandish.

3. Reverse Engineer the Rescue: For each item on the "failure list", brainstorm ways to prevent or minimize the damage.

4. The Reality Check:
   - Are some of those risks so great that the whole idea needs rethinking?
   Is it better to face this now, rather than after time and resources have been wasted?

Reflection:

- Gut Check: Was the group overly optimistic initially?

- Did we find some change champions who are secretly terrified and need additional support to feel confident moving forward?

- Key Takeaway: Smart pessimism is an act of self-preservation

Worksheet R5: The Permission to Pivot

Objective:

Embrace the mindset that adjusting the initial plan doesn't equal failure. In fact, it can assure success! Agility is key!

Steps:

1. Choose a project that needs to deviate from the original plan.

2. Analyze the Roadblock: Clearly define what's NOT working, avoiding blame and focusing on systems/processes.

3. The "What If" Brainstorm: Throw out wild alternative solutions. The focus is on quantity, not quality, at this stage.

4. Vetting the Madness: Now, pick the TOP 3 most promising alternatives and briefly look at the pros, cons, and what would be needed to implement each.

Reflection:

- Did anyone resist course correction initially? Why?
- Did the brainstorm uncover an unexpectedly simple tweak that could be a game-changer?
- Key Takeaway: Success isn't about rigidly sticking to the plan; it's about reaching the destination, even if you take a few scenic detours.

Worksheet R6: Reflection Knowledge Hub

Objective:

Capture + Celebrate achievements, challenges, and learnings in a Reflections Knowledge Hub

Materials Needed:

- Projector or large screen for presentations
- Whiteboard or flip chart
- Markers
- Reflections Knowledge Hub

Steps:

1. Before the workshop, review team achievements/wins, challenges, and learnings in the Reflections Knowledge Hub.
2. Schedule your Roundup!
3. Personal Stories: Invite team members to share personal stories related to work in the Reflections Knowledge Hub.
4. Future Goals: End the session by setting specific goals to use the learnings in the Reflections Knowledge Hub in the next two weeks/quarter.

Reflection:

- What can the team learn from the past quarter to influence future performance and engagement positively?

Discuss the value of collective reflection in achieving team goals.

Worksheet R7 Make Meetings Matter

Objective:

Increase Focus Time for Work by Killing Wasteful Meetings

Steps:

1. Ask everyone to look at their last month's calendar.
2. Create a sticky note for every meeting they feel was a waste of their time, noting frequency and duration.
3. Ask everyone to add up their waste!
4. Ask each person to share their results.
5. Add the cumulative wasted time.
6. Now ask everyone to share their top three time-wasters
7. Are there shared culprits? Quantify it.

Reflection:

- Can we eliminate these meetings from our calendar?
- Can we change the content, frequency, duration?
- Can you as manager help kill the meetings?

Worksheet R8 Look for signs of fatigue

Objective:

Being aware of change fatigue is an important part of understanding it, and then reducing its impact on your engagement.

Steps:

1. Get a leadership team together to reflect
2. Ask them to reflect independently and compare the answers to the questions below.

Reflection:

- Time to reflect. When a new priority is given to the team, do they pounce on it? If not, don't just assume this is because they are busy. Question, are we levying too much change onto the team?
- When last did we change structure? What level of comfort does the team have that the structure won't change again, or that they feel safe?
- Do people feel that the only constant is change?
- While leadership change and structure change may be necessary from time to time, stability enables people to optimize their workflow and improve their productivity. What can we do to create that stability? Several suggestions are in the workbook already. Showing empathy – acknowledging the reality of the amount of change and resulting fatigue for your people, and reducing the clutter of unnecessary or lower priority projects.

If the internal answers don't jump out at you, reach out to us for advice.

Case Study

How a Government IT Helpdesk Used Reflection to Stop Drowning in Tickets

Picture this: a government agency's IT department is perpetually caught in a tsunami of helpdesk tickets. Password resets, malfunctioning printers from the Clinton era, glitchy software updates forced upon them without warning... the classics. Urgent infrastructure modernization projects keep getting pushed back while they play whack-a-mole with a thousand minor annoyances. Morale is in the basement, burnout is rampant, and even the most dedicated techs are starting to feel like glorified reboot monkeys. That was the grim reality facing the IT team at a large state-level agency...**until they started reflecting in a way that led to change.**

Step 1: Beyond the Helpdesk Ticket Abyss

The usual "employee satisfaction surveys" were useless here. Sure, everyone was miserable, but those surveys didn't provide the granular data needed to pinpoint why. Here's how they got specific:

- Ticket Time-Sponge Audit: For one brutal week, every tech meticulously tracked where their time truly went – not just vague categories, but down to "15 minutes helping Sandra in accounting figure out why the 'any key' won't print."

- Problem Patterns: They took it beyond individuals to the systems they used. Were 60% of tickets due to a buggy new system? Was there a spike after specific software patches? Suddenly root causes started to emerge.

- The "Frustration Scale": Alongside each ticket, techs rated their frustration level, and why. Was it a simple fix but made infuriating by outdated documentation? This added a less quantifiable, but equally important, layer of insight.

Step 2: From Data Dump to Actionable Insights

Leadership's initial reaction was panic – the raw data was a horror show. But instead of finger-pointing, they focused on themes:

- The "Death by a Thousand Papercuts" Problem: Many infuriating tickets were minor, but collectively consumed vast amounts of time. Could they automate password resets, or create a user-friendly troubleshooting portal with those super basic fixes?

- Silo Suffering: Turns out, the recent software "upgrade" hadn't included essential training for IT, let alone end-users. How can the IT Helpdesk team and end users be included in the roll-out process to avoid messy clean-ups afterward.

- Hero Culture Backfires: A few superstar techs were single-handedly keeping the system afloat, while harboring massive resentment. Many were on the verge of quitting. Can we standardize knowledge sharing and improve documentation? What will happen if our heroes take their brilliance elsewhere?

Step 3: Reflection + Real Authority = Progress

The IT team's insights and proposed solutions only mattered because leadership was receptive. The sheer severity of the crisis forced soul searching at the top. Here's what changed:

- IT Gets a Seat at the Table: They were included in high-level planning meetings, not as afterthought, but to prevent those roll-outs that spawned a thousand helpdesk nightmares.

- Budget Battles: IT got a bit more muscle to push for necessary upgrades instead of being stuck in an endless patch-and-pray cycle. Were they suddenly flush with cash? Nope, but some strategic wins proved their point.

- Kill the Zombie Projects: A hard look at the backlog revealed projects that could be mercifully axed, or at least de-prioritized. This freed up brainpower for those truly impactful improvements.

The Impact (It Wasn't Overnight Magic)

- Ticket volume decreased. Not because citizens magically became tech-savvy, but due to targeted self-help tools and behind-the-scenes fixes that prevented common errors.

- Morale improved... cautiously. Suddenly, techs were fixing root causes, not just putting Band-Aids on a perpetually crashing system. This built a sense of agency lacking before.

- Proactive, Not Just Reactive: Could they anticipate the next roll-out disaster? Sometimes. This is where the strengthened relationship with other departments due to the improved communication became key for the IT team

Key Takeaway: In a government setting, especially IT, change is often agonizingly slow. But, by structuring reflection around actionable data points, and engaging a leadership team that is truly shocked by what was found, this department stopped drowning and maybe, just maybe, began to lay the groundwork for a 21st century IT operation.

Appendix

APPENDIX

Appendix

Making the Case for a Culture Shift

In today's fast-paced business environment, many organizations prioritize financial metrics, technological upgrades, or cost reductions. While undeniably important, these elements often overshadow the most critical competitive strategy: organizational culture.

Why Your Organization's Culture Matters

When culture thrives, employees are more engaged, teams are more cohesive, customers are more loyal, and businesses are more resilient. When culture thrives, organizations thrive!

Ignoring culture, on the other hand, can result in a disengaged workforce, low morale, and eventually, financial downturns.

Your Call-to-Action: Make the Case for a Culture Shift

To enact meaningful change, you'll first need to make a compelling case for a culture-centric approach within your organization.

Leadership across the organization needs to:

1. **Evaluate Current Culture**: Utilize employee surveys and interviews to assess the state of your current culture.
2. **Identify Pain Points**: Use the collected data to pinpoint areas that require immediate attention.

3. **Compile Benefits**: Research and compile the benefits of a strong organizational culture.

4. **Present to Leadership**: Create a compelling presentation to showcase your findings and recommendations to the organization's leadership.

We have launched an app to help you with these steps. Contact us for more information about CLOVER ERA

Appendix

WEEKLY PLANS

Weekly Plans offer a structured approach to implementing the Clover Framework in your organization. These plans help your team gradually adopt practices that boost engagement, making it easier to track progress and adjust as needed.

Week 1: Focus on Communication

Objectives:

- Introduce team to the importance of open communication.
- Begin implementing practices from the Communication section of the Clover Framework.

Activities:

- Monday: Kick off with a team meeting explaining the week's focus and planned activities.
- Wednesday: Conduct a "Two Truths and a Lie" icebreaker to improve interpersonal communication.
- Friday: Hold an "Open Mic" session where team members can share accomplishments, concerns, or questions.

Week 2: Dive into Learning

Objectives:

- Create awareness around continuous learning.
- Introduce team to Learning exercises from the Clover Framework.

Activities:

- Monday: Distribute a list of recommended articles, books, or online courses.
- Wednesday: Hold a "Learning Lunch" where team members can discuss what they've been studying.
- Friday: Allow team members to present a skill or piece of knowledge they've recently acquired.

Week 3: Unlock Opportunities

Objectives:

- Make the team aware of internal mobility and growth paths.
- Engage in Opportunities exercises from the Clover Framework.

Activities:

- Monday: Share an overview of career paths within the organization.
- Wednesday: Conduct the "Opportunity Mapping" exercise.
- Friday: Host an "Internal Mobility Fair" or invite guest speakers from different departments.

Week 4: Embrace Vulnerability

Objectives:

- Establish trust and psychological safety.
- Implement Vulnerability exercises from the Clover Framework.

Activities:

- Monday: Introduce the concept of vulnerability in the workplace.
- Wednesday: Conduct the "Vulnerability Circle" exercise.
- Friday: Run a "Failure Stories" session to normalize and learn from failure.

Appendix

Week 5: Enable and Empower

Objectives:

- Identify and start phasing out legacy practices.
- Conduct Enable exercises from the Clover Framework.

Activities:

- Monday: Discuss the importance of enabling employees for success.
- Wednesday: Engage in the "Process Mapping and Identification" exercise.
- Friday: Conduct the "Stop-Start-Continue" exercise to identify legacy practices to phase out.

Week 6: Time to Reflect

Objectives:

- Make reflection a regular team habit.
- Introduce Reflect exercises from the Clover Framework.

Activities:

- Monday: Share the benefits of reflection and mindfulness.
- Wednesday: Run the "Quarterly Reflection Workshops" exercise.
- Friday: End the week with a group "Mindfulness Practice" session.

Appendix

By following these weekly plans, your team will have a structured way to integrate the principles of the Clover Framework into their routine. This phased approach helps ensure that the practices for enhancing employee engagement are adopted in a manageable and sustainable way.

Appendix

MONTHLY REVIEWS

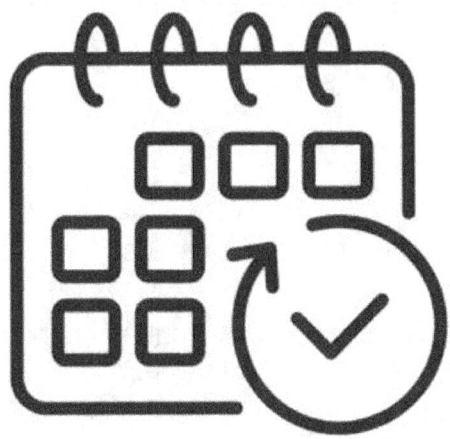

Monthly reviews provide an opportunity for your team to take stock of the activities, exercises, and cultural shifts implemented through the Clover Framework. These reviews are critical for identifying what is working, what needs adjustment, and planning for the month ahead.

Here's how to structure your Monthly Reviews:

Week 1: Data Collection

Objectives:

- Gather all relevant data and metrics on employee engagement.
- Collect feedback from team members on the past month's activities.

Activities:

- Data Gathering: Compile data from engagement surveys, performance metrics, and other relevant sources.
- Employee Feedback: Send out an anonymous survey to collect team members' thoughts on the exercises and activities conducted over the past month.

Week 2: Data Analysis

Objectives:

- Analyze the data and feedback to understand trends and areas for improvement.

Activities:

- Data Review: Conduct a deep-dive into the metrics and survey responses.
- Trend Identification: Identify patterns, improvements, or areas of concern in the engagement metrics.

Appendix

Week 3: Team Meeting and Open Discussion

Objectives:

- Present findings to the team and discuss openly.

Activities:

- Presentation: Share the analyzed data and feedback during a team meeting.
- Open Discussion: Allow team members to share their thoughts, ask questions, and suggest action items.

Week 4: Plan for Next Month

Objectives:

- Use the insights from the review to plan activities for the upcoming month.

Activities:

- New Objectives: Based on the review, set new objectives focusing on weak areas or doubling down on what's working.
- Monthly Plan: Create a detailed plan for the upcoming month, including specific exercises and activities from the Clover Framework.

Quarterly Add-On: Leadership Review

If the monthly review coincides with a quarter's end, include a Leadership Review session where team leads and higher management can discuss broader organizational strategies for employee engagement.

Objectives:

- Align team-level findings with organizational goals.
- Gain leadership insights into resources or policy changes needed to improve engagement.

Activities:

- Leadership Presentation: Team leads present findings and plans to higher management.
- Resource Allocation: Discuss the need for any additional resources or policy changes that could facilitate better engagement.

Monthly Reviews are not merely an administrative task but a dynamic process that should evolve as your team becomes more engaged. They offer a structured way to evaluate the impact of your efforts and make data-driven decisions for continuous improvement in employee engagement.

References

Introduction
Clifton,J. & Harter,J. (2023) *Culture Shock.* Gallup Press.

Communication
Porath, C. (2018) *Why being respectful to your coworkers is good for business.* TedTalk.
https://www.ted.com/talks/christine_porath_why_being_respectful_to_your_coworkers_is_good_for_business
Clifton,J. & Harter,J. (2023) *Culture Shock.* Gallup Press.

Learning
Senge. P. M. (2006) *The Fifth Discipline: The Art & Practice of the Learning Organization.* Doubleday.
Pink, D. (2009) *Drive: The Surprising Truth About What Motivates Us.* Riverhead Books.

Opportunity
Brim, B. J. (2019) *How a Focus on People's Strengths Increases Their Work Engagement.* Gallup.https://www.gallup.com/workplace/242096/focus-people-strengths-increases-work-engagement.aspx
(2022) *8 Employee Engagement Statistics You Need to Know.* HR Cloud. https://www.hrcloud.com/blog/8-employee-engagement-statistics-you-need-to-know

Vulnerability
Edmondson, A., (2023) *Right Kind of Wrong: The Science of Failing Well.* Atria Books.
Frei, F. (2019) *How to build (and rebuild) trust.* TedTalk. https://www.ted.com/talks/frances_frei_how_to_build_and_rebuild_trust

Enablement
(2011) *Does corporate culture drive financial performance?* Forbes. https://www.forbes.com/sites/johnkotter/?sh=392988491372

Reflection
Chesser, L. (2018) *6 Common Contributors to Uncomfortably High Employee Turnover Rates.* Zippia Official.
https://www.zippia.com/employer/6-common-contributors-to-uncomfortably-high-employee-turnover-rates/

Index

- **A**
  - **Actionable Take-aways** - Page 204
  - **Adventure-Themed Learning** - Page 81
  - **Ambition Roadmap** - Page 107-108
  - **Appendix (Worksheets Tools and Resources)** - Page 227
- **B**
  - **Behavioral Engagement** - Page 17
  - **Burnout** - Page 191
- **C**
  - **CLOVER Framework** - Page 16
  - **Communication** - Page 25
  - **Continuous Learning** - Page 64-67
  - **Cultural Shifts** - Page 234
- **D**
  - **Discretionary Effort** - Page 17
- **E**
  - **Emotional Engagement** - Page 17
  - **Employee Engagement** - Page 14-15
  - **Empathy Not Solutions** - Page 52
  - **Enablement** - Page 151

Index

- - Engagement Muscles - Page 10
  - Engagement Workbook - Page 9
- F
  - Fail Fest - Page 134
  - Feedback as Fuel - Page 191
- H
  - Hackathon - Page 169
- I
  - Index - Page 243
  - Inclusive Brainstorm Worksheet - Page 52-53
  - Internal Mobility Fair - Page 231
  - Introduction to CLOVER - Page 16
- K
  - Knowledge Sharing Not Hoarding - Page 168
- L
  - Leadership Advocates Rescue - Page 169
  - Leadership Learning Demo - Page 65-66
  - Learning - Page 63
  - Learning Journal - Page 79
  - Learning Mentor - Page 64
- M
  - Mindfulness Practice - Page 233

Index

- Monthly Reviews - Page 234
- N
  - 'Never Quit' Mentality - Page 11
- O
  - OUR WHY - Page 7
  - Opportunity - Page 85
- P
  - Pocket Guides - Page 72
  - Process Mapping and Identification - Page 232
  - Psychological Safety - Page 117-118
- Q
  - Quarterly Reflection Workshops - Page 233
- R
  - Reflection - Page 185
  - Reflection Hour - Page 189
  - References - Page 231
  - Reverse Mentor - Page 134
- S
  - Self-Improvement Ninja - Page 205
  - Skill-Swap Fridays - Page 69
- T
  - Team Dynamics - Page 191

Index

- **The "Pre-Mortem" Experiment** - Page 210
- **The Opportunity** - Page 106
- **Time Commitment Expectations** - Page 12-13
- **Transformation Initiatives** - Page 169

- **V**
  - **Vulnerability** - Page 117

- **W**
  - **Weekly Plans** - Page 229-234

www.ingramcontent.com/pod-product-compliance
Lightning Source LLC
Chambersburg PA
CBHW052246220526
45471CB00001B/212